Negotiation Skills

Skills

Avoid Negotiation Mistakes That Lose Your Contracts

(Secrets Of Power Negotiation And Better Business Relationships)

Allan Dawson

Published By **Jackson Denver**

Allan Dawson

Negotiation Skills: Avoid Negotiation Mistakes That Lose Your Contracts (Secrets Of Power Negotiation And Better Business Relationships)

ISBN 978-1-77485-888-2

Legal & Disclaimer

The information contained in this ebook is not designed to replace or take the place of any form of medicine or professional medical advice. The information in this ebook has been provided for educational & entertainment purposes only.

The information contained in this book has been compiled from sources deemed reliable, and it is accurate to the best of the Author's knowledge; however, the Author cannot guarantee its accuracy and validity and cannot be held liable for any errors or omissions. Changes are periodically made to this book. You must consult your doctor or get professional medical advice before using any of the suggested remedies, techniques, or information in this book.

Table Of Contents

Chapter 1: How To Be A Good Negotiator

This chapter will explain the importance of being a good negotiator.

Life is not about getting what you deserve. You get what it takes to get it. Chester L. Karrass

As we interact more with our family, friends and customers, as well as strangers and colleagues, there are many opinions, goals, needs, and desires that we encounter. Everyone wants things arranged according to their individual perspectives and terms. No matter how close or distant you are, your partner will always want the best outcome for their conversations and negotiations.

If we are not good at listening to our own needs and coming up with the best solutions for them, these differences in opinions, goals and desires will almost always lead us to disappointment and dissatisfaction.

1

Negotiating is part of our nature as humans. All walks of life will involve negotiations. We should be able stand firm in our beliefs and remain true.

This chapter will concentrate on fundamentals of negotiation, as well as the tactics that can be used to get the results you want. These fundamentals can help you become an effective negotiator.

Your Mindset to Negotiate

You bring your mindset to negotiations. This is just as important than the tools, tactics, and techniques. This is a key part of being a good negotiator. How you approach the table will impact the outcomes you achieve as negotiator.

A Negotiator's Viewpoint

A successful negotiator must always hold strong convictions that they stand by. Before you negotiate with someone else, it is important to have complete conviction in your beliefs. Uncertain of your own ideal outcome, you can't negotiate a deal.

Flexibility

The key to being a good negotiator is to keep things open-minded throughout the process. But they must also be aware of the limits of their flexibility. Flexibility can cause problems in your stance, and you may accept things that are not right for you.

The key to being a good negotiator is to be flexible with changes. A negative outcome is possible only if you are steadfast in your original negotiation. Understanding the tactics of your opponent and their tendencies can help you become a better negotiator.

Patience

Being patient is a key skill for negotiators. Negotiations should never feel rushed. You should also be patient. Rushing or hurrying negotiations can lead to serious mistakes and oversights. These mistakes will eventually stall negotiations and could lead to a result that is not realistic for you.

In addition, it can lead to poor presentations of facts if you rush the negotiation process. Don't make the negotiation process seem rushed. Make sure you hear all facts to ensure the best outcome.

Resilience in the face of pressure

Resilience is a key component of being a good negotiator. All negotiators need to realize that there are many tactics, tricks, or techniques their opponents could use to try and sway the negotiation process in their favor.

Negotiators should be aware that these tactics can change. They should also strive to maintain their resilience. Resilience when faced with pressure can help to break down any barriers that are preventing you from advancing your arguments and achieve a favorable outcome.

Indifference to Results

To be a good negotiator you should not attach yourself to any particular outlet. An attachment to a particular outcome in the negotiation process will always cause problems.

This can lead to a loss of ability to think rationally. In such cases, you may end up making emotional decisions which are not based on facts.

Emotionally Proactive

Effective negotiators must maintain complete control over their emotional reactions to the negotiation process. You could be at disadvantage if you make a mistake and you will lose your chance of reaching a good outcome. Stay emotionally detached throughout the negotiation process. Your emotions can interfere with your ability to make the right decision.

Essential Negotiation Skills

To become a better negotiator, you must learn the fundamental skills that will help you in your negotiations. You have already discussed the fundamental mindset changes that you will need. However, you must also be aware of the skills you need to effectively negotiate.

These skills include the following:

Communication Skills

Communication is the ability you have to speak, listen and persuade. These skills are vital and necessary for long negotiations. The best negotiation results can be achieved by listening, persuading. Writing and speaking correctly.

These skills are important for achieving a practical outcome. We all need to communicate on a regular basis. If you fail to pay attention during negotiations, your chances of reaching an acceptable conclusion are greatly reduced.

Listening

Although we will discuss listening skills later in this book, we will also share some information here. Listening skills are important for listening to what someone else is saying and for understanding what isn't being said.

The words people use to express their emotions and true intentions can often be seen. Listening well will allow you to pick up on all the key words as well as what they actually want to share. Listen to understand the other person, and then listen to their arguments to help you negotiate a good outcome.

Speaking Skills

Listening is not enough. It's important that you can communicate your ideas to the other person. So that the other person understands what your words are, it is essential to speak clearly and slowly. Use the right words. This will ensure that you don't misunderstand and that there is no double meaning.

To improve your communication skills, you can practice speaking to understand the meaning of each word.

Rapport Creation

To build positive rapport with your opponent, you can use speech. To build trust in negotiations, you must be both a good listener AND a great speaker. Both of these roles are important for gaining respect from your adversary.

Writing skills

Your writing skills will play a major role in any negotiation you do with someone, online or on paper. Your writing skills will influence how you are perceived by your opponent in such negotiations. You must be able communicate your points in the most effective way possible while building respect for yourself and your opponent.

Persuasive Ability

The communication variables listed above all contribute to your ability persuade. If you use these variables and are a competent speaker, you will be able to convince people to agree to your terms.

Ability to think creatively

Negotiators who are successful should be able and willing to consider all aspects of the negotiations process. The ultimate goal should always be to identify and explore potential areas of agreement, so you can uncover hidden opportunities or discover unexpected possibilities. There is always another way to think. This can allow you to think creatively and find that perspective. A new perspective can really help you in negotiations and can offer you new ways to ensure you get what is best for you.

Critical Thinking

To be successful negotiators, they must know how to critically assess the argument of their opponent and present a rebuttal. All arguments, facts and opinions that are presented by your negotiation partners must be critically examined. You will only be able to determine how they can change or favor you if you carefully examine their arguments.

Questioning Variables and Possible Outcomes

We now need to focus on the essential details that make successful negotiators. Each negotiation is made up of potential variables and possible outcomes that you can examine before entering into negotiations.

Consequences if you win or lose

Clear understanding of the consequences of winning and losing a negotiation is essential for you as well as the person you are dealing with. This will help you to understand your strategy better and develop a stronger negotiation plan. This information will enable you to make more informed decisions, be prepared for all the challenges, opportunities and obstacles as the process unfolds.

Possible Solutions

Not only should you know the outcome, but you also need to be aware of the alternatives that may exist for managing the situation. These options will allow you to find the next best solution if your preferred solution isn't feasible.

Think about all the possible options, and then decide who you will benefit most. The best thing for you is to consider all possible options. This will give you an idea of the best alternative solution.

Potential Trades

As we'll discuss in this book, there are always trades you could use to convince your opponents to abandon their original position. These trades can make or break your negotiation success. The trade you bring to the table doesn't necessarily need to have the same value for both you and your counterpart.

So that you can present a viable trade opportunity, it is essential to get to know your opponent's motivations. Knowing what your opponent might offer is a benefit.

Keep your mind open and consider all the elements of negotiations both before and during the process.

Chapter 2: Basic Negotiations Strategies

A Few Simple Strategic Points: Let's start with our personal strategy and work our way up. These are seven simple strategies.

Strategy One: Focus on Your Strength

* You believe that the deal which you offer is the best

* Your ability to solve problems.

* Your preparation. Your knowledge and prepa knowledgeable about the other side's needs.

Strategy Two: Be Patient.

* Act like you have all the time, but pay attention to clues that the other person's time is running short.

* Never rush a deal. It is better to "slow down" than to "jump in" when you bargain.

Strategy Three - Explore Options and Make Tradeoffs

* Both sides tend to find a more satisfying solution to conflicts when they examine their ideas.

A tradeoff should be valued by how it affects other issues and what you get in exchange. You should aim for a "quid pros quo" -- something in return for something. Don't be quick if you don't need the item. Don't forget to get what you promised.

* You should evaluate trades according to their value, and not by how many trade-offs they have. There are no requirements that you have equal trade-offs. However, you do not want to be the one who gets the lower end of the stick for the total value of all trade-offs.

Strategy Four: Personalize Yourself.

* Help the people on either side to see you as an individual. Tell them that you have feelings, problems and needs just like them.

This bonds makes it more difficult for them not to use you in the negotiations. Add to that, making yourself likable will increase your chances for receiving better treatment. It is easier to treat someone you like poorly or take advantage of them. This is not a guarantee. This lovely business phrase is worth remembering. This beautiful business phrase says, "It's Nothing Personal; It's Just Business." This phrase has served as the excuse for the most unethical and unprofessional business behavior.

Strategies Five: Building Bridges

* To build trust and continuity with your other expectation of ongoing contact.

* Establish bridges by keeping your promise of follow have promised.

Strategy Six - If it doesn't threaten the deal, you might consider compromise

* Even though I don't advocate compromise in all cases, it may be the best choice.

* Only compromises will be considered if you've tried your best to create a win/win solution that both sides can live with. You have most likely compromised if you are saying "It wasn't really what it was, but it was all I could get."

Strategy Seven - Recognize Dominators as well as Collaborators

There are four basic styles of negotiations. But there are also two common types of negotiators. To deal effectively with your opponent, you need to know which category they fall into.

* Collaborators work together to identify the needs of both sides and minimize conflict. Collaborators, unlike Dominators, enjoy building close personal relationships. They seek out solutions. Be aware that even if you have to deal with a Collaborator your interests are their primary concern. While they may be mindful of your concerns, they are not your representative.

* Dominators must be able to control people and the agenda. They are determined to dominate all relationships because they perceive others to be threats to their security or position. This is why you work to either negate them or to make them more conciliatory.

These questions are essential for your strategy.

Are these things worth negotiating? Is it better to negotiate this or do I have a better option?

Nearly everything can easily be negotiated, even though most people don't choose this route. You can negotiate many goods or services that most people don't consider. You can bargain at retail stores for goods and in medical offices for medical treatment. Some friends of mine will find something they like online and contact the company to inquire if they will match a competitor's price, or if the price will be reduced if they buy more. Amazon vendors will list the goods they sell and let you know if you want to get a discount or a coupon code to lower the price if you order multiple items. Many vendors don't encourage negotiation as they don't believe it would bring them any additional savings.

Are you willing to negotiate if the price seems low enough? Every set of circumstances will be different. I'll negotiate a case of an article, but I won't negotiate down any single item that they gave me the price of $1. I took my seven-year-old granddaughter to the flea market. I was trying give her basic lessons in negotiation. I asked her. "If they tell that the item is worth $1, and you are certain that it is more valuable than that, would you ask them to give fifty cents?" After a moment, she said she would not because that would have been insulting. I thought that she was a girl after mine. "If they tell you that the item is worth five dollars, but you know it's much more than that," she said. I was impressed when she said, "I would like to ask them if three dollars is enough." She would counter with three dollars and possibly get them to agree or counter with four. "What's the point of saying three?" I asked. I expected to be proud of the analysis. "Well. "Well. We will keep her.

Your strategy should embrace The Three Ps

Negotiations fail if the Pre-Requisites Three "Ps", Aren't Embraced by Both Parties

Negative beliefs can make negotiations halt before they even start.

Perception: If participants don't think the "playing ground" is equal, it will be difficult to achieve success in the process. Participants will believe that the process is unfair and won't lead to an agreement. If I believe the deck favors me, then why would I agree?

Preparation: A result cannot be achieved if participants aren't ready or are unsure of where they are at the moment. Participants who aren't confident they have all the information they need to make a deal can act tentatively and fear signing any agreements. Participants will not be confident about terms and will struggle to make the deal work.

People: There is no way to reach a consensus and trust without cooperation. Any proposal that is rejected by one of the negotiation partners becomes suspect. It is impossible to accept any information as truthful. Motives are continually being questioned. Explanations can't be trusted.

Your strategy should consider time related issues

In all the years I have been negotiating labor contracts, many of the negotiations were about time sensitive issues. It is time-sensitive language that demands bargaining when it comes to working conditions, salaries, and benefits. The Gambler, Kenny Roger's hit song.

"You must know when to hold'em

Yes that one.

Negotiating is often time-sensitive because of the delicate issues that surround the negotiation. When is it most appropriate to sell or buy an item? When is the best time to buy or sell a product? We shop sales that have a time limit. All of our warranties and returns must be made within the time limit. The shelf life of products are limited. When is the right time to buy a washing-machine? When is the right time to purchase that washing machine at the flea-market? Time for delivery, time to pay, time for warranty, credit terms, and so forth are all important in business negotiations.

Time constraints in negotiations, like in other activities are subject to an 80/20 rule: 80 per cent of concessions tends to occur during the last 20% of the negotiation time. Good negotiators keep their concessions up until the very end. They also preserve "throwaway items". These are items which are not meaningful to one side but have value for the other. It is possible for a concession to be of little value to one side at the beginning of the process to become a "sweetener" which seals the deal in the end.

When you should negotiate. How early you start dealing can affect your success. When you buy or trade something, you can capitalize on seasonal trends and market movements that may drive prices down or upwards. A purchase made on the downside of a supplier's business cycle can save you a significant amount. Do not buy automobiles or other items until the end-of-a model year. This is when salespeople are most eager to fulfill quotas and receive factory incentives. This requires that you do your research. If you incorporate time into your negotiating strategy, it could be your friend or your enemy.

Time is limited, so deadlines are inevitable. While you hide your deadlines, look out for these clues to see if the deadline on the other side is coming:

You can apply time pressure to move the discussion along or end a deadlock when it serves your purpose.

Your ability to control emotions must be part of your strategy

Some negotiators will attempt to humiliate you by making you swear, screaming or beating the table. Some will try to make you agree to a deal by playing the victim. These tactics can only work when there is a perceived power gap between the parties. The stronger side senses this, and will try to bully each other into making a deal. The bully will try to control you, but you have the ability to take back control. What can you do to weather the storm if you see it happening? You must take charge of your situation. There are a few strategies you can use.

1. My favorite way to wait is to wait till they are done. Remain calm and state your position as if you hadn't been spoken to. Since their attack was designed to scare you, this is fair. This is the calm and collected response to someone trying rattle you.

2. Another calm option is to jump right into problem solving mode. Both of our interests

need to be addressed if we're going to get a deal. Let's explore options that will deal with both.

3. You can fight fire by fire! You can get right back at them. I don't like your attitude or your proposal. If you really want to strike a deal, then change your attitude. I propose that we ...." They are admonished for their bad behaviour and given a brief reset about how to proceed with a new proposal or suggestion.

4. Only respond to your emotions if you have a plan. How convincing is your ability to fake hurt feelings or outrage. It can be done, but not everyone is successful at it. You can't do this with the same people all the time, so make sure you pick your spots. In 35 years of labor contract negotiation, this has worked for me only a few times. It is easy to tell when your team realizes you're faking it.

You must remember that allowing emotionalism to escalate will eventually lead to negotiations breaking down. You will leave the deal with severe prejudice. You won't want to do business again with this person/organization.

Your Strategy must be built around preparation, preparation and preparation

Information acquisition in the digital age is simpler than ever. The internet can be used to access information about people, companies, industries, or markets. You will be more confident when you negotiate if you have more information. Information is power. Therefore, information gathering is an essential part of the negotiation process.

Before you start negotiations, it is important to get information about the particular deal you are about forging.

Pre-Negotiation

During Negotiations

Your ability to ask questions and dig deeper into the negotiations is critical to gaining information. Ask questions that probe into the hidden agendas and secrets of the other side, such as what, where? when, how and why.

These questions might be answered by you talking with your competitors or customers, reading trade data or articles about the opposite party, and/or consulting standard business information sources. Also, you can ask insiders for information. This is the "as seen on television." You see this type of business intelligence gathering on television all the time. This can be used to help with business deals. Meetings were held to identify contacts who could provide us with information about clients and suppliers. Make sure you are thorough in your inquiries. This will ensure that you ask all the right questions and get a complete picture about the other person's true interests.

Chapter 3: Negotiation Techniques

Negotiating is a rare skill that every businessperson should possess. The only way to master this skill is through practice. You will need to use various tricks and techniques in real-life situations. Although you can't become a professional negotiator without making mistakes, you can still use books, articles and courses to help you. This is how I can save you from long hours and years of trial, error, and the pain of reading hundreds upon pages of literature.

Below, we'll be looking at ten highly effective negotiation techniques that have been proven to work by many professionals negotiators. Then, we'll talk about the conditions and rules that must be met in order to negotiate, as well the nonverbal aspect of negotiations and how to get the most out of your negotiation skills.

We're looking at:

Each one has more information.

Technique "Small moves"

The "Small Moves", a basic negotiation strategy, is one. It is a basic negotiation technique that allows you to monitor the effect of your actions on your opponent. You can do this by making small moves and then watching their reaction. Think about what you might say, for example to your interlocutor.

- Good afternoon! John Smith spoke to me not too long ago and told me...

The interlocutor might react differently, beginning with surprise and ending in irritation. He may not be able to remember John Smith's name or decide that you gossiped about John Smith. Better to say:

- Good afternoon! Yesterday was the last time we spoke with John Smith. The conversation turned to John Smith.

The next step is to wait for the opponent's response. You can enhance a move if you get something from your interlocutor like:

Ah, John Smith! Yes, Yes...

If John Smith starts to clarify who he is, it's better to stop developing the topic. This means that the interaction should be constructed slowly: start with a small beginning step, observe the reaction and then proceed to the next.

Technique "Power shoulder"

The "Power-shoulder" technique can only be used in situations where one party has the ability or power to influence another's decision. You can illustrate this technique by using the following metaphor:

A turtle is swimming through the river while carrying a snake. The turtle believes that it can drop the snake and bite it. The snake believes that it can bite the turtle.

If one side is aware that it has a stronger side, you can forget constructive negotiations. There will be negotiations of a manipulative nature in which the strong enemy presses the weaker opponent, waiting for him to start retreating, or power negotiations with an pronounced WIN/LOSE strategy.

Technique "Inner Observer"

The "Internal Observer", a technique that allows you to influence the negotiation process but only if there is constant monitoring of your opponent to see which negotiation strategy he prefers.

If you are subject to psychological pressure and you still try to compromise your desires, this will be perceived weakness.

Be alert and on guard during negotiation. You can use your internal observer to help understand what is going on and keep an eye out for the moment when constructive negotiations turn into destructive.

Technique "If", instead of "No."

Many believe that "No" is the only rule in business communication. However, many people are mislead. Expert negotiators use the phrase "If ...".."

"I will cut the price a bit if I purchase two ...".."

"If I buy the camera, will you send me a protective case?"

Remember, a person saying "No!" has a lower chance to win than someone who answers all questions with the phrase "If ...",", and those who use the phrase "If ..."" often get a bigger reward than what they initially calculated.

Technique "Empty Cabinet Method"

The "Empty Cabinet Method", commonly used in negotiations, has the goal of lowering the price or reducing the cost for a contract. The technique's meaning is to mentally open a cupboard in front of your opponent. This will show that you don't possess as much money as he requires.

You love the $5000 price tag, but you aren't able to afford $3950.

This is a common tactic used by sellers to make concessions. You don't have the right to accept any small discount offered you by the seller. Remember, you only have $3950

Technique "The gun should always be loaded."

The "Guns are always loaded" technique is a reflection on the main hunting principle. According to this principle, the hunter always treats the gun like it is loaded, even when there are no cartridges.

Think of it as if your opponent misunderstands you. Or, in some other way, the opposite. Then, prepare to take specific steps to resolve this issue (think about an action plan).

If, after negotiations, it becomes clear that your opponent is not understanding you or doesn't fully understand you, you will be prepared for the situation. You will have a plan and a loaded gun.

Technique "There's no fixed price"

Market economies are where the "There is no fixed price" technique comes from. This topic is well-known. Prices are determined by how supply and demande are related, as also how much the buyer would like to save.

Make the rule of bargaining one of you rules. It could be about completely different areas or topics. Bargaining can be acceptable, legal and expected. The purpose of price tags is to place on you the price policy that best suits the seller. You can offer your price and the seller may refuse.

You can get much more out of bargaining than if you just follow the suggestion of your seller (or opponent).

Technique "One-gate game"

The "One gate game" strategy states that you cannot make concessions, or make any special offers, until you are ready to bargain. Any concessions you make or special offers you make will result in a concession from your opponent. His offer should be more lucrative than yours.

You should accept any concessions made by them and then continue negotiations as if nothing has happened. Your primary goal in negotiation should be to accomplish your goals.

The technique presented is harmoniously combined with "If" instead "No."

Technique "The method that principled man uses"

Technique "The principled man's method" can help you achieve your goals and minimize losses in negotiations. The principled person is the one who allowed you to take part on your own in negotiations. You can also act as a principled individual by your boss, friend, or relative.

When you negotiate, you must let your opponent know that you are representing another person and that you have certain conditions that you can't change.

In most cases, this tactic puts your opponent at a standstill and forces him to agree with the conditions you have set. This technique can be used against you. You can ask your adversary to link you with the person who is negotiating.

Technique for tough guys

The "Tough Guys" tactic is used when negotiations take place with the tough guys.

Keep calm when your opponent screams, threatens or trouble you. In no situation should you enter into open opposition. You must not give in to emotions and avoid arguing about matters that aren't relevant to the negotiation. The "tough" guys will eventually "go limp" and will be more open to compromise.

Never forget that, no matter what your opponent does, it should not affect the outcome of negotiations.

These negotiation techniques may look very easy on the surface, as they do not contain many complicated actions or clever "spy" tricks. It is important to remember the simple truth that all the most important aspects are always visible on the surface. You'll find that the simpler the technique, both in terms of how easy it is to use and how skillful you can negotiate.

You shouldn't think that everything can be done in a single day. This is a huge mistake. It must adhere to specific conditions and rules if it is to be effective.

Chapter 4: Negotiating Among Multiple Groups

Most often, negotiations take place between two parties or two people. You may, however, be called upon to join negotiations with multiple parties. You will need to perform additional tasks in this type negotiation. Let's suppose you are in charge. These are the tasks you should do.

1. As you've conducted the bilateral negotiations, you should also be following the basic steps.

2. Make sure everyone knows the location, time, day, and date of the negotiation.

3. Each participant must be provided with a copy and acknowledgement of the ground rules.

4. Each negotiator must be assigned a role during negotiation.

5. In order to make the environment more informal, each participant must introduce themselves before starting the negotiation.

6. The arrangement must allow negotiators to see each other.

7. Each group should be met and gotten to know before they can negotiate. Although you may be friendly with them, they must follow the rules.

8. It is important to establish order as soon as possible. Let them know who's in charge. But be as helpful and supportive as possible. This will let them know you are willing to lower their anxiety and make it easier for negotiations.

9. A large number of participants means that there will be many ideas and concepts to choose from. It is important to be able to mediate during power struggle.

10. You should be aware of potentially volatile situations. If this happens, it is crucial to be able and willing to help.

11. Ask them questions. Listen intently to the answers. What are their expectations and goals regarding the negotiation? From their responses, you can make your own judgment. However, you must suspend judgment if your information is incomplete.

12. It is important to be able identify their personalities so that you can monitor them and discern who might be difficult or easy for you to convince.

13. Activities that aren't well organized can make it difficult for multiple people to work together. They must be allowed to manage their own ranks. For each group, designate a leader. The leader will ensure order and consistency during negotiation.

Negotiating with multiple people: steps

Step 1 - Learn more about each party

Know everything about each party and the negotiation. Get to know them well by meeting them prior to the actual negotiation.

Step 2: Justify your stand and show support

Present your proposal and justify and support it. Encourage them to ask questions in order to explain to them what you believe.

Step 3 - Give them the opportunity to present their proposal

Ask relevant questions to find out why they are standing for what they believe in. Ask them what they want to achieve and what their objectives are.

Step #4 - Find a solution with them

It is better to have multiple heads than one. So, discuss the issues and come up with a solution. Discuss ways you can come to a compromise. With everyone's cooperation, you can definitely reach a solution.

Step #5 Finalize your contract

Finalize any agreement. Get the contract prepared and signed by all of you.

Step #6 – Implement the contract

You are now allowed to implement the contract. To make sure that everything goes according to plan, you will need to monitor and ensure that all terms are being adhered to.

These steps are very similar, however there are many more tasks.

Chapter 5: Negotiating For Success: Basic Phase

Each person engages into negotiation. We bargain together with family members on vacation arrangements; we bargain among friends about who pays for dinner; and with contractors, when the delivery or repair will take place. Physicians can bargain with patients about medical or surgical therapy. Scientists trade for experimentation space. We all negotiate for our salaries, and our job responsibilities. While each case presents its own risks, these examples all require basic communication skills for effective negotiation.

Richard Shell defines negotiation, in his book Bargaining to Advantage (Penguin Books 2000), as an interactive communication procedure that happens when someone wants something from you. Shell divides this process into four phases.

Preparation

Exchange Information and Discussion

Bargaining

Closing and Engagement

This book discusses the four phases of negotiation using everyday interactions among faculty members in negotiations for new positions within business schools.

Phase of Preparation

A great negotiation preparation process involves spending enough time thinking about what you want, the alternatives to your current deal, and the potential value that our counterpart might bring to it.

Never let yourself be swept away by a critical negotiation. It takes a lot of preparation to negotiate well. It takes time to assess your objectives, negotiate position, and consider the alternatives.

Leigh Thompson of Northwestern University advises negotiators to conduct a deep self-assessment in her book The Mind and Heart of the Negotiator. She suggests that you ask the following questions during negotiation preparation:

1. What do you want from me?

2. What is my backup strategy if we cannot reach an agreement with each other?

What do you want?

Thompson's initial question demands that we identify an ambitious goal but one that is achievable. Thompson suggests three traps to avoid in setting a goal.

You must avoid being an inexperienced negotiator that sets unrealistic targets. Avoid setting unrealistic targets and you could fall prey to the "winner's curse" which refers the disappointment experienced when the other side accepts our offer. The fact that the other side is open to accepting your initial offer shows that you were too optimistic and didn't adequately prepare for the negotiation.

It is not a good idea to be too ambitious in negotiations. If you set unrealistic goals and refuse to make significant concessions, then you will be left without a contract.

Another issue is when you haven't done enough preparation to negotiate that you are unsure what you want. Negotiators are often suspicious of good-faith offers from the other side.

What is my backup strategy if we cannot reach an agreement with each other?

To improve your chances of reaching an ambitious but realistic goal, you need to first identify the best alternative to a negotiated deal, or BATNA (Best Alternative To A Negotiated Agreement), as Roger Fisher and William Ury recommend in Getting there: Negotiating Agreements without Giving In.

The BATNA value will allow you to decide whether or not you want to continue the project. Deepak Malhotra from Harvard Business School and Max H. Bazerman, Harvard Business School, note that the BATNA Assessment involves three steps:

1. List all options you have if you can't reach an agreement with the current party.

2. Calculate each alternative's value.

3. Determine the best option, also known as your BATNA.

The first step for job seekers who are preparing to negotiate a specific job offer is to research other job options and other options. This could include staying at their current job or applying for graduate school. The second step would be evaluating the monetary and non-monetary benefits of each alternative, including expected salary, benefits and engagement in one's work. This analysis will assist the job seeker in identifying her preferred alternative.

Calculate the Valuation of Your Reservation

Once you have identified your BATNA via negotiation preparation, you can calculate the reservation value (or reservation price), which is your walkaway point in the next negotiation. It can be a particular number in a price negotiations. A package may be used to express your reservation value in an integrative negotiation.

It is possible to avoid making two errors by knowing the exact value of your reservation.

1) Accept a worse deal than your BATNA

2) Turn down a better deal than your BATNA.

Evaluate your Counterpart's BATNA

It is important to not only focus on one's personal needs and wants while preparing for negotiations. You need to assess the willingness and ability of the other person to help you make a mutually advantageous deal. To do so, you must conduct a BATNA analysis.

The following question should be asked: "What will the other party do if we reach a deadlock in negotiations?" It forces you to think about the other side's reservations value. The job seeker might conclude, for example, that the hiring company has qualified candidates ready to take the job at low salaries. This could lead to the job seeker realizing that he has little leverage over the hiring manger when it comes to salary negotiations. The job seeker may also recognize that she is one the few qualified candidates to fill an open position. In such cases, she may negotiate for a better deal.

Preparing for negotiations must start with an objective assessment. The more organized and systematic you are in your negotiation preparation, the better your negotiations will turn out.

Discussion and Exchange Information

It is the most critical step in the negotiation process. 1978: A study of English labor- and contract negotiators who conducted actual transactions revealed that successful negotiators asked twice so many questions and spent twice the time clarifying and acquiring relevant information than average negotiators.

Numerous observational studies in 1978 have proven the crucial importance of these basic communication skills for effective negotiation. Henry Ford spoke highly of such communication. He said, "If there is one secret for success," that it was "the ability to see things through the eyes of another person as well as from your own." These interpersonal communication skills are crucial in this type if interaction. Shell speculates that people are so grateful for having an attentive audience that they will ignore your tactful probing until it becomes compelled to seek out answers. This is when the skilled negotiator has all the information required to give the correct answers.

Timothy Johnson interviewed various people in the medical school and department during his search for the University of Michigan chair of obstetrics. A vision and planning document of 18 pages was created from the conversations and reflections on what could be built in the medical school. This document shared the visions and potentials of both the department and medical schools. The shared interests and common ground of those with whom he would develop the vision made it easy to reach an understanding. How did he come to discover common interests, and the possibility of creating a great division? It was by asking questions, listening, clarifying, and cultivating shared interest.

Phase of Bargaining

Bargaining is the stage that most people associate it with. However, this stage does not constitute a stage in negotiation. It begins with a discussion on terms, followed by the beginning of the discussion about a "deal". Dr. Steve Blum teaches AAMC EDS members to put off this stage as long possible and recognize when it occurs. He says that you can shift from information exchange into bargaining as soon as one party mentions a number or term. When negotiations have been managed well and reached the stage for information exchange, this transition happens naturally. It is a natural extension to how to implement the new ideas. If the exchange goes well, both parties will have likely discovered alternative solutions that are better than the original ideas.

Additionally, both sides are more likely to be happy with the final transaction if the discussions are approached with the best-case scenario. When negotiating, it is important to think positively. Legend has it King Ching, the Chinese King of Chou, said that high achievement comes from lofty goals in 12th-century China. Think about negotiating in a way that meets mutual needs. One must be prepared to understand the bottom line and Best Alternatives to a Negotiated Agreement. (We'll be covering BATNA further in a subsequent issue. Understanding one's personal values is essential to avoid losing them. A good deal will leave everyone feeling they gained or lost little. Spend enough time before you get to the negotiation stage. This allows you to come up with common values and mutually beneficial ways of exchanging ideas or property.

It was through effective negotiations with people from diverse backgrounds that significant curriculum changes were made across the country. The "bargain", which is used to boost visibility of one department in return for greater integration or dispersed teaching, is commonly used. This can involve negotiating a new system of allocating funds to department to recognize teaching efforts, while also taking into account the effects of these distribution methods on budgeting of divisional and departmental levels. Each of these are the results of a bargaining effort that contributes to a wider vision of effective teaching, learning, organizational innovation, and other benefits.

Chapter 6: You Can't Win Every Battle

When trying to persuade others, one of their biggest errors is to assume they must win all battles. This can quickly become an obsession. You need to take time to fully absorb and then accept these profound and important ideas. Although you may lose some battles on the way, it should not hinder your long-term plans of war. Too many people are too fixated on their short-term strategy, becoming argumentative and dogmatic over any minor disagreement. Their determination to win every game can lead to a loss of trust and credibility as well as the possibility of weakening relationships and connections. For the overall prize, you must be ready to give up some ideas. Do not be upset if you lose smaller points.

It is common to hear, especially in marketing, that you should be aggressive in pursuing your goals. I don't believe that this is a long-term viable strategy. It can lead to short-term wins, but it does not offer long-term credibility or connections. This could be detrimental to the goals you are trying achieve. Persuasive individuals tend to have a long-term view of their situation and to recognize that any short-term gain could be detrimental to their position. The temptation to create an urgency can backfire. A person who is rushed to do something will likely become bitter after reflecting back and looking back at the meeting. This works well if you are only trying to persuade people in a one-off situation. However, it is not a good idea for the long-term.

For over 60 years people have been studying the traits that are most prominent in influential people. It is a powerful opponent to be able demonstrate an in-depth understanding of the circumstances you face and to have an understanding of others' opinions. You might be better off waiting until you are able to understand both your own and the opposing viewpoints before trying to convince them that your choice is the best.

While logic can be very appealing, emotions can sometimes dictate the decisions people make and the direction they go. Negotiators will need patience to learn what drives these emotions and find a way to placate them. But it is worth spending the time to overcome your emotional objections in order for you to be persuasive.

Each case, every persuasion attempt is only part of a larger picture. Keep your precious, hard-earned credibility. It may take time to build your reputation, but it is easily destroyed. Keep it in your sights above all else.

Chapter 7: How To Implement Bargaining: The 7 Principles Of Principled Negotiation

Identifying and identifying interests

Fisher and Ury say that the first phase in principled negotiations involves identifying the stakeholders involved in the problem rather than trying to negotiate the positions. This distinction is critical in the integrative school. The central focus of distributive bargaining is the position or stand of the parties. However, the interests explain the individual positions.

Integrative approaches insist that in order to negotiate effectively, parties must move beyond the boundaries of their interests and try to fulfill their essential needs. So, negotiators can approach issues of common concern with greater understanding and flexibility. While interests are more easily identified than positions, they can slip under the radar or be concealed behind a party's position or demand. Participants may not have defined their fundamental interests in a prudent way.

People

This is the other element. According to researchers, disputants often forget that people on the opposite side have people who share their values and are susceptible to human frailties, such as emotional misinterpretation, wrong assumptions, and misunderstandings, when trying to achieve their goals. It is crucial to separate the problem from people. This is about finding a solution that doesn't get sidetracked or influenced by the individual elements. Also, it means that everyone will be able to agree on how to keep the relationship going.

This is a way for the parties to collaborate more and easily share information. There are good chances that the parties will reach a win/win solution. Good relationships can be built by the parties using strategies that allow them to get to know each others better. This could be staying on in negotiations, meeting informally, and making time for a chat.

To ensure that negotiators feel respected and respected by the other party, they must be mindful of essential strategies and considerations. This could include taking steps to ensure no participant feels compelled to compromise their own views or appear weaker because they have accepted the demands from the other party. Negotiators need to recognize that protecting their dignity shouldn't be so important to the negotiation that this obscures the significance of the key issues or creates deep conflicts that could impede or delay progress towards an accord.

Alternatives

In order to establish a realistic target, negotiators should ask themselves important questions like where each side will be after reaching an agreement, and what other strategies they have to achieve the goals they set if the other party is not cooperating. In integrative and distributive-based approaches, it is important to pay attention also to substitutes. Integrative approaches, however, seem to place less emphasis on concepts like bottom line and reservation points when negotiating with positional strategies. They are more open to substituting for other parties. It is important for both the parties to have a clear understanding of their BATNA – Best Alternative to a Negocated Agreement - both before and during negotiations.

Identifying your options

Once the parties have built relationships and begun exchanging information, so that they are more clear about the interests in the balance of power, they can start to think of alternatives. In negotiations, preferences can be considered feasible solutions to problems shared between at least two parties. Options can be used to reach as many interests as possible in integrative negotiations.

The orange story demonstrates that when two entities, (companies and nations or individuals), get stuck in routine patterns or solve problems, they quickly lose sight of the possibility of creative thinking. It is vital that the process of recognizing possible solutions, or options, to a problem stimulates creative thinking. The process of brainstorming allows for the creation of options. This is a technique that asks all parties to not only note new ideas but also to criticize them. It encourages creative thinking and increases the chances that everyone will come up with a solution.

Communication

Fisher and Uri both noted that communication was essential in order for negotiations to succeed. Emotional support is another important aspect of negotiation. Effective communication skills are key to changing attitudes, preventing misunderstandings and helping to improve relationships. It is essential to communicate clearly and effectively with the other party.

Integrative approaches emphasize the importance and value of information sharing.

This is a way to expose interests and aid parties to identify common threats or issues. However, communicative incompetence and blunders can hinder negotiators from fulfilling their roles. One example is that parties can become too focused on their own reactions and lose sight of what the other party to the negotiation has to say. Listening is a great way to learn about the other side. It also shows you are listening and paying attention to what they have to say.

Fisher and Ury promote active listening as a means to improve communication skills. This means listening to the other party, not to give a reply but to learn about them. Paraphrasing without agreeing, constantly conceding what was or was not said, asking questions, and paraphrasing are all great ways to show your attentiveness or active listening.

Criteria or Legitimacy

In order to negotiate a compromise, one side will have to give up his original claim. The practice of negotiating in which two parties are locked into disagreeable positions is known as "positional bargaining". This can lead in conflict of interest, deadlock, and bitterness. They maintain that negotiations can be costly if parties approach them in this manner. For instance, positional negotiators may finally come to an understanding that "divides the differences" between their opinions. But, a more rationally composed answer would have been more in line with both parties' interests. It is possible to make agreements in this way difficult to use if the parties decide later that they do not want legality. But there are other ways to approach negotiation. This includes using objective criteria to guide negotiations.

Commitments

An agreement can only be lasting if all of the parties respect the promises they made. Rejecting the promises of the other party will lead to their resentment, loss of integrity and possibly even the termination of the agreement. Even those who were not in the deal (in the unlikely event that they make public any information about their reputation) will refuse to sign any future agreements with them.

It is not a good idea for either side to make pledges they won't honor. Fisher and Ertel believe that each party should consider the types of commitments it is willing to make in the course of negotiations. They can honor them. How long can they be expected to honor their promises? What commitment should be so far-reaching?

Research has shown that trust can only be built by establishing a framework for implementing commitments in phases. Parties might be more willing to work with rivals if it is possible to show that each party is keeping its promises. How can parties be rehabilitated if their trust is broken? Gestures can be used as a way for one party to regain trust with another party after they have lost their integrity due to past bad-faith acts. One example is that a party that has failed to fulfill a contractual obligation may have to make advanced payments on a contract to convince the other party they are worthy of doing future business.

Key Strategies (Ways to Become an Effective Negotiator)

Numerous individuals and groups have experienced success by using a "more natural" approach when negotiating. These people don't fuss, make noises, or try to force their way into difficult situations. An effective way of negotiating can be as natural as a natural way. How does it work? This chapter will cover 21 strategies that can help you become more effective at negotiating.

Strategy #1: Be aware about what you're willingly accepting

You don't always have to plan ahead for negotiations. However, it is possible to avoid making a big mistake by knowing when and where you will accept the terms.

Strategy #2: Accept that negotiation is vital

Negotiating is both exciting and stressful. Sometimes you might not like this idea. Remember that negotiation is essential in order to achieve positive results in your decisions.

Regardless of how we feel about it, we all negotiate. If you ignore it, you will lose. It is common for people to try to cause harm to others. But these people do only what is in their own best interests.

Strategy #3 - Explore new things

You don't have to feel uncomfortable or irritable when you negotiate. Focus instead on trying new things or doing things out of your comfort level. To achieve desired results, it doesn't take to be a skilled negotiator.

Strategy #4 - Find someone who can assist you

Take into consideration that not everyone you approach when negotiating is available to handle every situation. Don't assume they have the time. If that happens, approach politely others.

Strategy #5 Never dismiss someone on a negative note

Remember to include other parties in negotiations if necessary. Tell them that they are important to you and that you are happy. You should also mention why you feel the need to reach out to other parties in order to avoid confrontation.

Strategy #6

This is an important strategy, but it seems that most people forget about it. If you ask permission to use other people's names, it will not cause any disputes between you and those individuals.

Strategy #7. Don't be afraid asking open-ended questions

These are just a few examples of open ended questions. You can't negotiate if you answer yes or non without additional explanations.

Strategy #8. Look for other options

Many places offer secondary options, reduced rates, and all other types of discounts. Some cases won't allow you to determine which option exists unless your ask. In negotiations, there is always more than one solution.

Strategy #9 Demand for the things you want

It's true that the world is a better destination for great people. Many people are too busy working and trying to find what they want for their families (and themselves) is a common problem. People ask for help. If you show them the way, they'll follow your lead.

Strategy #10, An ultimatum can be a big no!

Be clear of words like "I require 30% off, else I won't sell anymore!", "Take it or leave" or "This is my final deal." It isn't fun for anyone to be told what to do.

Strategy #11: Don't be too vague

To make negotiation more difficult, stop fumbling about. Instead of trying to dictate what you want and expecting too many from the other side, ask for the desired outcome with clarity.

Strategy #12 Listen to the First - It is a common saying that negotiators have that who speaks more during negotiations loses. Bobby Covic (author of "Everything can be Negotiated!"), says trust is built by listening first. It is possible to satisfy all parties by simply listening well during a negotiation. It can be difficult to listen and pay attention to what the other party is saying.

Strategy #13: Talk less, listen more

Talking too much is not necessary when you are negotiating. Talking too much can lead to regrets. Silence can make some people feel awkward. Talking less can mean making fewer mistakes, which is something we don't want while negotiating.

Strategy #14. Start negotiating by finding common ground, making positive compliments, and talking about your mutual interest

Talk about something you enjoy together before you start asking for what it is. It is best to approach the other person and talk about a shared interest. This will allow both parties to relax and let the conversation flow. Say, "I would like you to talk about this important issue, but I first need to hear your side."

Strategy #15. Don't take any negotiations personally

Although you might be able to get what you want, it is unlikely that you will be able establish good relations with others by taking things personally. You should not make arguments when the other party speaks objectively. You can respond to what they say by making your own suggestions. It's a no no to personal attack on the other side!

Strategy #16 Respect people

When negotiating, it is important not to jeopardize relationships, burn bridges, or make others feel disrespectful. Give respect, and you'll receive respect.

Strategy #17, Walk away from bad reasons

There may be things that you are uncomfortable hearing or saying in negotiations. In these cases, it is possible to walk away. Experts believe it is okay to walk away if the reasons are clear to both parties.

Strategy #18. Know the best time to close a meeting

If the other party is closing the deal soon, your role will be to make it easier for them put into action all aspects of negotiations.

Strategy #19

If you don't prepare, a negotiation will not work. Plus, you may be aggressive for wrong reasons.

Strategy #20. Consider the objectives of other parties

Emotional motivations may be a factor in negotiations depending upon what was agreed between the parties. You need to focus on the objective side rather than their emotions to negotiate a deal.

Strategy 21: If the opposite party made a first proposal/offer to you, define parameters for your negotiation

When negotiating, be open to gauging your response and setting parameters. While some experts recommend that your proposal be the first to the table, this strategy can be advantageous for all parties.

Strategy #22: Plan your flow of proposals/counter-proposals

This strategy will give your negotiation skills more scope.

Strategy #23 - Sit Down – This tells the other party that they are going to spend some time listening or negotiating. If you do not have enough time to listen, don't ask the other person to speak.

Strategy #24: Move in towards the conversation and lean in Head nods and head nods let the other party know they are being followed. Hypocrisy will be displayed if you do not stop nodding or keep repeating the word "right".

Strategy #25, Keep Your Cool. Generally speaking, all experts agree that these are the best ground rules to avoid communication problems. No yelling or walking away.

Strategy #26: Be Specific - Billikopf suggests that you should be concise and straight to the point. The parties must avoid words such as "we disagree" and other phrases that would put one in a defensive situation.

Strategy #27 Avoid Empty Threats You will lose the respect of others by threatening them with empty threats.

Strategy # 28: Forget Neutrality. Shapiro says that trying to control your emotions usually backfires. The other person can sense your frustration and anger through your wrinkled foreheads, tightened mouth and tone. Negative emotions will always cause problems in negotiations. You should instead ask for positive emotions to be expressed.

Strategy #29 - Don't yield - Billikopf said that although it might seem noble, giving up on important issues can lead to a breakdown of a relationship. He recommends not asking the other party for their opinion but to seek out compromises like stretching.

Chapter 8: How To Negotiate With A Friend

A friend is someone who will support you in whatever decision you make. Friends still have their limits. These limitations make it difficult to find the right way through everything you want.

Negotiating with a friend is more straightforward than negotiating with any other person, including family. You can still succeed if you follow certain negotiation methods and stay with them.

30. Make use of the power and repetition

Repetition works great in advertising and sales (see Chapter 3), and the same applies when negotiating differences between friends. Your friend must adapt to your outlook, style, opinions, or principles. Although you can't force a friend to adopt your style, opinion, principles, or outlook, you can use your influence, either directly, or clandestinely.

If a man wants his friend who is into football to also like skateboarding, this would be an example. It is important that they talk about it. He doesn't want to make the other mad, but to show how much they care about football. Also, it is a great idea to gift football items and souvenirs. It's also a great idea to bring a friend along to a football game, where the celebratory atmosphere creates a new moment, giving football a personal touch.

The friend who loves skateboarding may eventually try football. Either because he is passionate about the game or just to keep the friendship alive. In this scenario, the friend who pushes further and harder will win.

31. Give your friend the impression that you have the upper hand

Feel like your friend is your lifeline, your last hope. A cup of coffee and a donut are not the easiest things to negotiate.

It is more than just a reward. You should offer something greater: a boost in your ego and a triumphant feeling. Make your friend feel that you are owing them a lot. It is far more expensive to repay someone you love than anything else.

32. Refrain from asking for a nod

For negotiations in which you hold the money, it's better to ask than to request. Money can buy patience. You don't have to indulge your ego or accept your diva ways. But a friend might find it too demanding because it puts an end to equality in the relationship (unless they are the queen Bee, which, in the first instance, does not require negotiations).

No matter how intentional the step is, a friend who has been stepped on will typically defend his/her pride. This can make it difficult for you to negotiate. Try to ask as politely and nicely as possible.

33. Your friend should be in the mood to make your move.

Be kind and understanding to your friend when they need you more than you. If your friend is not feeling the need to be kind, attentive, funny, and follow you, then he/she probably needs someone to just listen to his/her rants. This is your chance to play the BFF.

Once your friend is over their dark clouds, this is the time you can grab the chance. Because a true friend always agrees to a friend asking for a reward, If you've been trying for years to get your friend their signature bag, it is time to make a move and reap your rewards.

Chapter 9: Effective Ways To Improve Your Negotiations Skills

Avoid making too many compromises when you negotiate. Negotiation does NOT always require compromising or bowing to other parties' wills.

For the best results, make sure you understand the other person and try your best to convince them to accept the deal as-is, rather than compromising.

You should highlight the benefits of your offer according to the person's wants and needs.

Perhaps you could compromise on minor points that won't be too significant?

Be different - You might find similar products and/or services offered by other companies at the same or lower prices than yours.

You should explain to your partner why you offer a better solution than others. This can only be achieved by conducting thorough research ahead of time. It is important to be able to influence others and make your case convincingly.

Listening is an essential skill during negotiations.

This is because people don't want to buy from vendors that aren't attentive to their needs.

Research has shown people who are not heard carefully feel neglected, unimportant and unloved.

Listening can be accompanied by three basic levels. Selective listening means that you only listen to the important things, responsive listening means that you give feedback to your partner physically and verbally. Playback listening allows you to repeat what you've heard to ensure that he is fully understanding and is really listening.

You need to make plans in advance of the negotiation.

Prepare a list of possible talking point, with objections and with rebuttals.

Success in negotiating requires certain elements

It is possible to use basic negotiating skills. But how can you deal with situations that keep getting more complicated?

This complexity is when multiple people are required to assist in the situation.

This is why it becomes a nightmare when negotiation moves from 2 people to 3 people.

To put it another way, negotiation becomes more difficult when each person puts all their emotion and effort into getting what they want.

One example is salary negotiation.

International Negotiations

Negotiation across cultural boundaries or international negotiations is a niche area in the negotiating field.

The basic skills of negotiation are irrelevant because such negotiations require more preparation.

In such cases, the negotiator will need to adapt the negotiation approach to suit the culture of the country where negotiations are taking places.

This knowledge is essential to understand how foreigners deal with one another in terms of their attitude, business etiquette and customs. It also requires an understanding of how they deal with conflicts.

Every country has its unique body language.

Before beginning the talks, make sure you do your research on the country's customs. Learn key phrases, read the guide to travel, and view movies while you are preparing. It is important to act as a native, respecting the customs and behavior of that country in order to close the deal.

Negotiations between Women & Men

It is now easier and more efficient to communicate between women and men than ever before. This is due to the fact that women are now involved in politics as well as big business. We can't deny that there are fundamental differences between them.

Negotiation over the telephone and the internet

Technological innovations have changed how people communicate with each other. This is thanks to the growing use of internet and phone.

The internet and phone make communication easier and more efficient than ever. You can now communicate with anyone from any location, be it your office, home or car.

However, such negotiations lack the personal touch through gestures, body languages, and human interactions.

When you have face-to face interactions, it is crucial that your body language matches your words.

If you are unable to do this, you should investigate the cause and take immediate action.

This could make you appear weak or insincere.

Element that influence the negotiation process

The smooth operation of negotiation can be affected by many factors.

This is key to a successful negotiation.

Some of these factors include:

Negotiator- The success or failure of any negotiation depends entirely on the skills and ability of the negotiator.

In the influence of the parties to the process, credibility and character play a major role. This is because the negotiator has a primary duty to control the entire process.

You must have the ability to be positive about the deal you are looking to make.

Parties - The success of a negotiation is also affected by the way that the parties involved react and respond to it.

This is because if people have different views or ideas, they might not be able solve the problem effectively.

Selection of team members - This must be done based upon the situation and specific cases.

Each individual must be capable of contributing to the achievement and promotion of pre-determined goals.

Location of negotiation - Because unfamiliar sounds and surroundings can cause stress, it is imperative that you choose the best location for your negotiation.

Space layout- The layout of the room must reflect the environment where they work regularly. Also, they should feel comfortable.

You must also ensure that the seating arrangements allow for communication. The position is an important factor in power play.

You should not have too many people between you.

Psychology in Negotiation- Psychology in Negotiation refers to the psychological strategies that are employed in different activities. Each person is different in how he approaches and perceives different activities. It is important to recognize these considerations and take action.

This is directly linked to the needs and wants of an individual, which are classified under:

Setting goals and planning to achieve them

First, set your goals. The next step is to prepare to achieve them.

Clear communication is key to your professional and personal life.

* What are the boundaries of your territory?

* How far you're willing to go in order to get th

* What will others not allow you to do?

* And so on.

Many people lose their way and blame their negotiating skills. It is likely their inner game or the wrong values that are keeping them from achieving success.

In this arena, you have to be ruthless at times.

To be more effective in negotiating, you need to create a master plan. This master plan contains strategies to help you make your dreams a reality. Only you need to make a commitment to controlling the most important areas of your life.

Be proactive, not reactive. Your vision must be created

Many businesses are successful because they have a vision or mission statement.

These statements might be found on their websites and printed in their publications.

While they work for the company, all employees follow the same vision/mission. Personally, however, they have no mission statement. For a life of success, one should have a plan. Clearer your goal, the more likely it will be to facilitate negotiations and vice versa.

This may seem trivial or big-picture. This is an important point, especially for negotiation and sales teams. They are the face of the company to all other participants in a meeting.

They should be in line with the company's vision and mission.

Below are examples of vision statements for some well-known and successful businesses:

Microsoft - "Someday there will be a computer in every home and on every desk"

Young businessman - To climb the corporate ladder honest and professionally.

My law firm - "To assist my clients realize there dreams."

Envisioning your future

Write down your mission statements to make it easier to realize your dreams. To start to think about your goals in your life, sit down with your partner.

While you are doing this, do not listen to what others think of your plans. Don't let past failures get in the way of your future success.

What is the point of all this?

Remember that YOU are always part the communication and therefore the bundle. You might be interested in this offer. However, if the negotiator or company rejects them? They will choose to work with someone else. It shines also in your sub communications like confidence and convictions.

To overcome your past failures, you need to work against yourself. If you don't, it will be difficult to predict the future.

You can try to separate your emotions (resentment. anger. and worry.) from the events.

Although emotions are human and natural, it is possible to control them once you become aware of them. Acceptance is the key.

Here are some suggestions:

* What are some of your talents?

* What are some positive qualities you have admired in your life?

* What are your targeted goals for the next 3-5 years?

* Would you like to see your legacy passed on to family members, communities, etc. ?

* Are there any doubts about your ability to meet challenges and take the responsibility?

* Things that you should avoid

* Hobbies, volunteering, spirituality, career, learning, etc. that you are interested in pursuing in your spare time. ?

* Where would it be nice to be if you could see yourself differently from where you currently are?

These questions are helpful in creating your mission statement.

It is important to make a commitment

Commonly, commitment can be described as a promise, pledge, or binding obligation. Although it's easier to commit than to keep, it's not always easy to carry out.

If you want to be lean, for example, you need to change how you eat. It's important that you commit to this!

Identify your core values

Values are the core ethics, standards and principles of an individual's existence.

It is your deeply held beliefs and attitude, as well as how you communicate with others.

In other words: Values in the negotiation sense are defined as your behavior and expectations towards others.

You can plan ways to achieve your vision

After creating your mission and understanding your values you must be clear about what you want.

It is important to have a clear vision of your goals and objectives in order to realize them.

It is not difficult for renown companies to translate their vision into reality, such as McDonald's.

Blockbuster was a rental cinema store that didn't have an adult section. Parents thought it safe enough to send their children to get movies there.

Many internet providers use parental control blocking to instill predetermined values into their businesses.

This has made it easier for parents to feel confident that their kids aren't watching porn online.

The 3 Year Plan

A 3 year plan is an important part of planning for both your personal and professional lives.

It also contains a backup plan. After three years it is possible to lose 100% of what you had planned.

However, if you do not have a clear vision of your future, you will continue to drift along in life. People who don't achieve their goals fail to look ahead and create a solid plan.

Consider the following when planning your 3 year plan:

Chapter 10: Preparing For Negotiations

Negotiation is an important part of daily life and all businesses. Because negotiation is an integral component of our lives, we often negotiate every day even though we don't know it. We can only make the right deal during negotiation. This is our turning point in every aspect of our lives. It impacts our lives, businesses, as well as everyone around. In any negotiation, we either win or lose. Learning the skills and techniques necessary to negotiate is crucial. You must also be ready for the negotiation. How far you'll go in any given negotiation is determined by how well you prepare.

It is essential to clearly define your goals, what you can afford, and what you do not want. You must also be self-confident, positive and optimistic. Without preparation, it is possible to give more than you get during a negotiation.

Personal Preparation

It is essential to get rid of tension before you enter into negotiations. Remember that there is nothing you need to worry about, as long your position is well understood. You must be polite and firm before and during negotiations.

Not being polite will reduce your argument. Being polite will not reduce your argument. It will actually lead to mutual understanding, and more effective bargains. If you have a bad perception of someone, politeness will help them to see you differently. You will make them more flexible if they have prepared for a tug to war with a defensive device. Because you are a friend instead of an enemy, they will be willing to sacrifice some things. A firm attitude will also help you to avoid the appearance of weakness. It is possible for the other side to mistake politeness for weakness by assuming that you are only showing politeness and not taking a firm stance. It is important to clearly define your objectives in the negotiation. Be firm about your position.

Your temper is the most frustrating thing in negotiation. You won't be able to come to an agreement with the other side if you or your partner lose your temper. You must remain calm. This is the best rule of any negotiation. You can persuade your counterparts until they agree to a deal by remaining calm.

Last but not least, don't take any negotiations personally. Never involve your family or your personal interests in negotiations. Sometimes, it is tempting to confront someone on the opposite side of a conflict. Avoid this situation.

Understanding that you are not clear in your position is a weakness during negotiation is also important. It is crucial to protect your position. If you are a member of your team, then no one else can know your position.

These steps will help you prepare to negotiate.

What do you want?

This is the most important part you need to work on. This is not a place to generalize your goals. Instead, you should have a clear line about what you aim for. It is possible to write down the things you want on a piece or paper. You should keep this in mind when you are going to negotiate.

It is important to know what you do not want. On your paper, you should have two columns. One column should represent what you want and one that describes what you won't accept. These will be the objectives of negotiation, so you need to stay focused on them. These two principles will give enough confidence to be able to negotiate your deal. It will help you avoid making mistakes and causing dissatisfaction.

Know your fellow sexy

Know your counterparts' personality. Find out how they live, how much they like to eat, and how they communicate. This will enable you to approach them, and you can negotiate for their interests. You should also be capable of reading their body language. This will help you anticipate their intentions. You can even offer to give something you like in exchange for what they want.

Know your counterparts' needs

Although you should know exactly what you want, it's equally important to know what your rival wants. This is an old strategy for winning battles. Your enemies are your best friend. This will help you create ways to defeat them. Your chances for winning will increase.

Know your counterparts' needs. Write down the things you think they might want and the things they would like to avoid. Once you know their goals and objectives, you can begin to identify commonalities and come up with a practical solution. You can leverage your opponent's weak points to reach an agreement if he is the counterpart. If you're in a partnership, try to weigh the weaknesses of both sides and come up with a mutually agreeable deal.

Identify possible concessions

Before you start to negotiate, you need to know your limits. These decisions will be made based on your goals. Both sides should agree to part with something in return. A win-win outcome should be the goal of any negotiation. You will both be happy with the deal if you do this.

Learn about your options

Analyzing all options is as important as knowing what you want. This will help you feel confident and will make it less difficult to negotiate a deal. Ask yourself questions when you are trying to negotiate for a contract on raw material. Can another supplier offer me the exact same services or products as I need? Is it possible to create these items yourself? Can I get help from anyone else at the company if I'm not getting a great deal with the current representatives? You can be sure that your comparison is accurate by asking the same questions. This will enable you to compare the strengths and weak points of all the options.

Rehearse

This sums everything you need to know about successful negotiation. It's as simple as that: practice, practice and practice. It is important to practice the skills and methods you will use, as well as what you don't like.

If you feel that you are not qualified for the job, it is possible to attend training sessions about negotiation. Negotiators are prone to overlook this step. This can make it difficult for them to get the results they desire in negotiations.

Weigh the consequences

You should be able see what the consequences of not reaching an agreement. The best way to find solutions is to do thorough research.

What effect will it have on you, your company, or your job if you trade something for another? Ask these questions before you enter into negotiations.

In this chapter, we'll be looking at various methods you can use to negotiate.

Chapter 11: How To Speak Persuasively, Not Abrasively

Communication is fundamental to life. There is no doubt about that. Communication is essential for people to communicate and exchange ideas, knowledge and to give life and shape the world. However, we take so much for granted that it becomes a problem. In fact, we've seen how easy and simple it is to misunderstand and misinterpret others without knowing why.

In the previous chapter, we discussed the importance and ways to improve your listening skills. We'll now be looking at effective expression because communication is both a process of receiving and expressing information. Now that you know how to listen, how do you speak? Without these skills, it is impossible to negotiate.

4.1 Confidence Is Everything

Even if everyone wants to have negotiations in good faith but remember that everyone has their agendas.

It is important to be open-minded, friendly, and willing to compromise. However, don't push the envelope: the lions are ready to strike at any sign weakness.

Transparency is key. However, it's important to be honest about your intentions and your goals. Keep your vulnerabilities and concerns close to your chest. Do not tell another party that you depend on them for success, progress or security.

These factors are invariably used against you during negotiations to make your compromises more difficult than you want. Maintain a calm attitude, speak with confidence and don't panic. If you are confident, you will feel the exact same. Don't allow anyone to overpower you.

While everyone admires and likes confident players, no one wants to do business in business with weak players. Be confident, but don't let your arrogance get in the way of your confidence. You want to look smart and successful, not bold and proud.

4.2 Crosscheck For Clarity

The last chapter discussed the importance and necessity of crosschecking meanings or interpretations when listening to others.

It's important to verify that the message being received is the same one as that sent.

People are not mind-readers and may not understand everything you say. Keep it simple and clear. You can always go back to the key points to make sure you're on the safe side. Clear speech, concise sentences, and no jargon are all you need. Watch for nonverbal reactions in the room while you speak. Once you're finished, ask questions.

4.3 Be clear about what you intend and what your expectations are

You need to be clear about your expectations during negotiations.

So everyone can understand the situation, communicate the same to them.

The answers to these questions can help you guide and make sure there is no confusion or disappointment in your expectations. It is important to be clear and concise from the beginning in order not to offend or disappoint the other party. Be clear and not inadvertently misleading.

4.4 Communicate Objectively

It can be difficult to remain impartial and fair in a world where everyone is trying to promote their cause. But, without objectivity, negotiations are almost impossible to achieve fair results.

Everyone at the table understands that everyone is there in order to meet their conditions. It's not necessary to stress the same through subjective speech, selfish behavior or overemphasis.

Look up and take the higher road. Pay attention to everyone's needs, not your own. Avoid using subjective pronouns and egocentric dialogue.

4.5 Use Inclusive Linguistics

It is an easy mistake to speak in a way that emphasizes what you want, and this can have a negative impact on negotiation and persuasion.

There are more risks than giving the impression you're selfish and childish (which doesn't cause enough damage), but it can also create divisions, and exclude others from the negotiation process.

When more than one party is involved, there may be shared interests and similarities that are discovered or highlighted. If this happens, the use of problematic language can cause members to band together against another. Knowing the difference between convincing someone or bullying them is key. Even though there may only be two groups involved in negotiation, it's important that they use language that emphasizes similarities but respects differences.

Use language that reflects your understanding that you're all part of the same team and that the cooperation experience is something all of you can contribute to and benefit from.

The logic behind this is simple: if anyone feels excluded from the process, they will not invest in its success. If people can be assured that they will be supported to the end, they will put forth their best effort. Alienating people through language is something we do almost every day without even knowing it.

Negotiating is a great way to ensure everyone feels valued, involved and acknowledged.

4.6 Aggression doesn't equal passion

You should never lose sight of your manners, regardless of what happens.

It is not pleasant to be spoken to in a threatening or aggressive manner.

You must be committed to the process and grateful for it. Remember to be considerate of your own actions when expressing your needs. You can feel strongly about a topic, but it is important to keep your cool.

4.7 Express Your Willingness For Compromise

You want people to believe that you are willing to negotiate with them. If you refuse to compromise and collaborate, it is impossible to achieve this. This ebook reaffirms the fact that sustainable success in negotiation is possible only with a win/win situation.

It is essential to recognize that not everything can be yours. It is essential to win over your opponent by letting them know you understand the situation and are happy about it. Communicating your willingness to compromise must be done with care. Clear, unambiguous and respectful language is necessary to assure others of your willingness to compromise.

Be aware of their concerns about your attempts at hijacking the negotiation.

Do your best for allies and not enemies.

Be clear, you're here to find a solution.

The quicker everyone realizes that they have nothing and everything to win by working together, then the faster you can get this process moving.

4.8 Respect Rational Limits

Let your imagination run amok during negotiation.

Your expectations must be reasonable and pragmatic. Even if you do manage to attract a long-standing competitor or an elusive businessman, that doesn't mean you should abandon your restraint.

Be realistic and cautious with your words, expectations, or appeals.

No matter if you are asking for discounts or looking for ways to sweeten the deal with something, remember that everyone has their own interests.

If you come off as being too opportunistic, this will only make you lose the chance to get another opportunity. They are unpalatable if they are exploitative.

4.9 Make Demands, Not Requests

It's the worst thing you could do during negotiations.

Nobody wants to work for a brat. Everyone deserves to be there. Respect that fact.

You should realize that any concessions you make are at the discretion, not just because you want them. Professionals should earn their victories, not expect to be treated well. There is nothing that screams "unprofessional" as clearly and disgustingly as making demands during negotiations.

Chapter 12: Meal Prep To The Busy Entrepreneur

We see food as a tool for changing and manipulating our bodies when it comes to weight loss, leaner, and fitter.

We lose the core idea of food in this way. The connection we have to food is to nourish and sustain the body. This not only impacts your waistline but also affects your mental and emotional health.

The psychology of eating is all in connecting our emotional and psychological state to the entire experience. When we nourish and fuel ourselves, we nourish our minds as well as our souls.

The term diet refers to manipulating your body or forcing it into starvation mode. A diet can be a way to live.

Food should make you feel good. You get bonus points if it tastes delicious and also nourishes your body. A negative experience with food can lead to negative feelings.

Preparing meals is a way for life. This is a type of diet that emphasizes healthy and nutritious home-cooked meals as well as portion control.

Psychology of Meal Prepping

Meal prepping teaches us how to make better and more conscious food choices. This improves our relationship with food. Meal planning also helps you to control your binging and compulsive eating.

It takes a lot of time to make your food. You pick your food ingredients, go to the market, cut, peel and dice your vegetables, and then move on to sauteing.

These steps will allow you to be in control of your appetite by preparing food. While it can seem daunting initially, and you may have to go through many hiccups, the end result is that you made a good meal.

Cooking and taking control of a task makes you feel calm and alert.

Meal prepping changes many deep-rooted, unhealthy relationships with food.

What are the factors that influence our eating habits and how can we change them?

Experts believe that there are many factors that influence our relationship with food and how we eat.

These factors include:

Many people use food to deal with their emotions, such as depression, anxiety, stress and boredom. This works well for short-term mood relief but can eventually lead to guilt or regret. In order to suppress these feelings, we end eating more. This leads to more negative emotions. As we gain weight our self-image suffers.

What role does psychology have in meal planning?

Psychology studies the psychology of behavior and examines why people behave the way they do. Psychology studies are useful for people who want to lose weight, or gain muscle.

* Behavior – Determines the person's eating and behavioral patterns and provides a plan to change them.

* Cognition (thinking - Therapy is done to identify self-destructive thought patterns that contribute to eating disorders or weight management.

When we get involved in meal preparation, we are more attentive to the food and take more pleasure in eating it. It is tempting to eat these foods, but it becomes boring once we are satisfied.

Meal prepping helps us be more grateful, mindful, aware, and appreciative about what goes into our stomachs and where it came.

How eating right and meal prep make you a better businessperson

Even though you might not believe it, good nutrition and meal preparation can help your business. Here are some healthy habits that famous entrepreneurs use, which you may find inspiring to try.

Seth Godin - A bestselling author and blogger, Seth makes the exact same breakfast every morning: a smoothie made with almond milk, frozen bananas and hemp powder. It doesn't mean you have to do the same thing every day. However, it does help to have a routine. A personal blender allows you to make smoothies on the go if you are limited in time.

Victoria Beckham, Fashion Designer and Entrepreneur, Singer, Model. -She is a staunch follower the Alkaline Diet. This diet promises to boost energy, improve memory, reduce heart diseases, bloating and insomnia. For alkaline boost, she begins her day with a glass warm water with lemon juice. After that, she continues to eat raw food and avoid refined sugar.

Martha Stewart, a businessperson and a writer. Her diet plan includes green juice every day, plenty of organic vegetables, and a preference towards a fish-based diet.

Sundar Pichai CEO of Google-Sundar, is a vegetarian who starts his morning with toast, an oatmeal for protein and tea.

Mark Cuban, Shark Tank host, and billionaire-commits to exercising at least one hour each day. He consumes smoothies as well as yogurt in his pre- and post-workout meals.

One of the greatest benefits of meal prep is:

You will invest in your own health

Meal planning allows you to plan the meals you will be eating each day. People who meal prep have a better chance of eating cleaner and more healthy foods than those who do not. Healthy food options are more likely to be available so you're less likely go after bad foods.

You'll have more willpower

Preparing meals helps you to get organized and you will eat healthy more often. It will be easier to eat healthy when you prepare meals for lunch, dinner, snacks and breakfast. It will also make it much easier to avoid binging.

It will decrease stress

Anxiety can also be caused when you wander aimlessly through grocery stores. It can be stressful to not know what to eat every day. Stress can have many effects on your mind, body and soul. Stress can affect your digestive system, disrupting your sleeping patterns and affecting your immune system. Meal prep will prevent you from asking 'What's for Lunch or Dinner?' Instead, you will reach for any pre-prepared food that is in your fridge. Heat it and then enjoy it. You and your family will be able spend more time together, have more fun, and have better food.

This will allow you to save time.

Only a limited amount of time is required to plan, prep and cook your food, as well as pack it. Once you have done this, you can spend less time in the kitchen. Your only responsibility is to cook and heat your food. It is not necessary to know what to make every day. This leads to last-minute trips to the shop each time you want something to cook.

Chapter 13: Four Principles Of Negotiation

Principled negotiation is a different type of negotiation. It involves four important steps that can help reach agreements to your advantage or get a deal on your terms. You will find four principles in this document that can help you resolve any type of conflict. These four principles are discussed below. These principles can be applied at all stages of negotiation and the strategies should be used throughout. This will ensure that negotiations are peaceful, constructive, and interactive. It involves the analysis and examination of a problem as well as the consideration of the views and needs of the other party. Finally, the mutual agreement between both parties creates a solution and negotiates a deal.

Alienated People and Their Problems

First and foremost, to get a no and work in your favor, you need to be free from the issue. You may find yourself getting so involved that it becomes personal and/or too personal. All your responses can then be viewed as personal attacks that will damage your egos. This is a big reason why your relationship with the opposing party gets worse or damaged. Because of this mentality, you tend to feel hurt and take a more negative approach. To win an argument, you must think calmly, without being defensive and with a positive attitude. It is possible to keep your cool and not take any issue personally, which will help you think rationally. All differences between the parties, conflict in interpretations, etc. require that both parties are decent enough to understand each other. It is possible to trust each other and place yourself in their shoes, which can lead to some of the most successful decisions for both parties. Blaming and blaming others is not the answer, especially when it comes to business. This makes the situation more difficult and can lead to poor relationships. It can bring you a lot of benefits to be understanding and even acting when dealing with problems or negotiating a deal.

119

Emotions should also be kept out of business negotiations. Do not get emotionally involved with the deal. People tend to be reactive and angry when their interests or those of others are at risk. Being able to manage emotions and keeping them out can help you win respect during negotiations and lead you to the right decision and solution. When relationships are strained and there is an emotional component to a deal, it can cause a war between emotions. Even if you see the other person as emotional and reactive, it is better not to react in that way. Instead, use the emotions to your benefit. To calm down the other party, make gestures or apologizes. You must be an experienced negotiator to understand that being emotional during a deal can lead to a bad relationship.

Communication is one reason why business negotiation can lead to problems. Communication is key in business negotiations. The negotiator must not only communicate his requirements and deal out, but also listen to the other party. By listening to other parties, you can get their insights and avoid any misunderstanding. If you fail to properly communicate your problem and your deal or if you are not heard correctly, then it is likely that you won't get a correct decision. This is true even if you are not the one hearing correctly. Many people focus on what they have to say, rather than listening to the other side. The best negotiator, however is the one who listens first to understand the other and then makes the decision about what to say. By listening to the other, you can satisfy him or her without making any compromises. In business meetings and negotiations, the speakers must remember that politeness is the best way to get your desired outcome. Being rude, offensive, or playing the blame-game will not get you far. Instead, it will cause chaos and make everyone angry. Keep things cool. This is the best way for you to get things done. If you want to reach a consensus or a yes, don't see the other side as an enemy. Instead, view them as a partner.

Find Your Interests and Get Clear

In order to negotiate effectively, it is important to clearly define your own and the interests of the other party in order for you to come up with a solution which both benefits them. But, to make things work in your favor, or to your advantage, you must be selfish and fight for your rights. Your interests should be at the forefront of your priorities. However, you shouldn't be rigid. Never be afraid to accept new ideas or opportunities. Be open to new possibilities. In business, it is not uncommon for one party to offer a cheaper deal than you. Be open to communication, and make sure you are flexible to adapt to new situations. This is how negotiations can be made to work in your favour. Diplomacy works in the same way as international relations. The principle that the nation's interests are superior to all others is used in negotiations in business. Your company's interests and your personal interests must always be the main focus when you make a deal. To reach an agreement, however, you should not compromise on your own interests. You must listen to the interests of the other person in order to make things work. The best negotiator focuses on his or her own interests, is open to hearing the other side and is open-minded to any changes or proposals but does not compromise his position.

You can create options

Third principle: Create alternatives to negotiate a successful deal. Sometimes, there are no alternatives and the parties agree to a deal. Negotiating is essential when there is conflict of interests. However, both sides should remain open to discussing other options. Sticking to your demand will lead to deadlock as the other party won't compromise on your terms. For you to win, you have to let go of some control and be open to negotiation. You don't have to agree to everything that is in a contract during negotiations. This is seldom the case. You must create options that suit both sides and reach a beneficial deal. Make sure you have options and alternative ways to reach the same goals, and be flexible to make things work in your favor.

In order to create an informal environment and ease everyone's minds, you can make the oddest or most bizarre choices when considering options. Critical thinking is essential to help you create your options and alternative that are in your best interest. Don't be afraid to use alternatives and positive offers. Otherwise, you will lose trust in the other party. Your business will not survive without the support of other businesses and good relationships. Neglecting to negotiate deals in a professional manner can cause havoc for your business and future prospects.

Use Objective Criterion

To negotiate, use legitimate and practical criteria and make informed decisions that will benefit your interests. To get a positive outcome, you must avoid rigidity or stubbornness. Explore the perspectives of the other party to attract their attention. It might not be beneficial in the real world, but it could work in your favor.

Chapter 14: Setting The Scene And Style

Once you have weighed the position, established objectives and assessed the nature or the arguments of the other side, your attention can now turn to the detailed planning of actual negotiations. Important is the general tone that will be used - assertive, assertive, formal or informal, declarative or rapid? The degree to which one side can dictate the style and arrangement of the room (seat plan, layout, etc.) is dependent on the other party's willingness to share the responsibility. You need to allow for the possibility that one party might have an alternative plan. However, most negotiators do not seem to pay enough attention to such factors, giving an advantage for those who do.

Six elements are required to be considered, though they are more important for formal negotiations between teams than informal discussions between managers. These points are:

The style or tone

If both parties agree to the win/win approach, negotiations will be friendly, cooperative, and constructive. It is best to place more emphasis on solving the problems together than on winning debate points, unless the other side is known for being aggressive. It would be a pleasant thought if this style were universally accepted and thus always appropriate.

However, such assumptions are not possible in reality. Sometimes, alternative styles are required in certain circumstances. Take this as an example.

Infintex is a computer agency that has a contract for a 3 year period to provide a costing system and wages for Zoxcot (a glazing company). The contract was in force for ten months. Infintex received a recent letter from Zoxcot, advising them to immediately terminate the contract. They claimed that the system was not meeting specifications. Infintex challenged this assertion: While there were some minor problems, the system was not in crisis.

Infintex was informed by industry sources that Zoxcot are facing financial difficulties. They intend to reduce their labour force and return to manual wage systems. Infintex will now file a written claim for compensatory damages due to breach of contract. Zoxcot can counter-claim the alleged cost of system failures.

Zoxcot's offices organize a meeting to try and reach an agreement. Based on previous correspondence, the Infintex teamwere not surprised to hear Zoxcot's managing director launch an unpleasantly aggressive attack upon Infintex's competence. He states that he has tabbed a string of system breakdowns and will sue Infintex if they don't drop the claim.

Infintex should prepare for an aggressive opening while planning for this negotiation. They need to avoid being provoked into a threatening rejoinder and must establish quickly that they have a strong claim and will not be forced into surrendering their claim. Zoxcot can be called on his bluff. Zoxcot's statements are an ultimatum, not negotiable, and unless Zoxcot are willing to discuss the entire position constructively, there's no point in going ahead with the meeting.

It is common to find a less dramatic, but more routine situation when talking with managers or negotiating with non-professionals like shop stewards. Negotiations can either go constructively or combatively depending on the tone in the first few moments. These situations are where the skilled negotiator aims to create a collaborative atmosphere and breaks the ice with some friendly general talk before opening up for discussion.

Whom should I involve

Informal managerial discussions are typically between one individual and not between groups. But one-to-1 bargaining is not always the best option, particularly if one person is dominant or has more experience in negotiating. The less confident manager should consider including another person.

Leo was a young, recently appointed personnel manger and wanted to talk with May, a cynical 55-year old divisional head, in order to convince her to consider psychometric tests when selecting graduate trainees. Leo had already had a disappointing conversation with May regarding another topic. His ideas had been ignored and little discussion ensued. Leo said this to May when he called her to arrange a time for them discussing tests. He also added, "I'll bring Bert Robinson, he can help us with cost information." Bert was one Leo's section heads. The real and effective reason Bert was involved in this discussion was to decrease the dominance May could attain in a one-1 discussion.

In industrial relations it is not unusual to see the trade union side field a large team. Perhaps a union official supported by a shop-stewards committee. It would be foolish for one manager to try to negotiate alone with this team. Negotiation requires concentration and quick thought. It is very difficult for one person in a negotiation to pay full attention and pick out every nuance. It does not necessarily mean that the manager team must be as large as the trade union staff. In fact, it is possible to have poor coordination between members of the team and for there to be divergent views within the team. Most experienced negotiators favor three or fewer members of a team.

Also important is the composition of a team. It's important to know how your team will react to unexpected problems. For wage bargaining, an example of a management team would be the personnel manager supported by two staff members. If there is an impasse, then a second, more senior team might be used. This could include the managing director (or finance director) and the personnel manger. In order to maintain continuity and prevent any misquotations from either side, it is important that at least one person participate in both stages.

Every member of the team should be thought about.

As an example, a three-person team might:

* One will assume the leadership role and take a constructive, problem solving stance.

* An additional party will follow a more difficult line, challenging the assertions of another party and generally pointing to the difficulties caused their claims.

* The third person can act as the 'sweeper,' watching other members' reactions, checking progress, and reporting back any points missed.

Pace and timing

Timing and pace of negotiations can have a huge impact on the outcome. A fast-moving dispute about a sensitive issue can lead to a tense atmosphere. You need to be careful when trying to resolve such situations. It is easy for a dispute about safety regulations to be turned into a second dispute over the management's perceived time wasting or reluctance talk. The best way to proceed is by suggesting to the other that both parties engage in fact-finding exercises before formal negotiations can begin.

In certain other situations, delays may lead to higher final settlement costs. This is especially true in wage bargaining when inflation is high. Numerous companies reached quick settlements in 1989 by offering immediate 6 percent offers (considered to be high at the moment). However, others who offered 4'12% and then became bogged down with protracted bargaining ended up paying 8/9% or 9/% when inflation increased.

Similar principles apply to managerial and commercial negotiations.

It has become a standard strategy in civil actions to recover damages or compensation for their clients. Lawyers will engage in prolonged correspondence before reaching an agreement on out-of-court settlements.

One theory is that the claimants might become so frustrated by prolonged delays that they eventually agree on a modest settlement, just to bring the matter over to a close. This tactic is clearly questionable in moral terms. It may also be an ineffective tactic.

Blatant time-wasting and determination of the claimant may be a factor in his or her determination to succeed.

The decision on whether to move at a slow or fast speed is one that each case must make. But, there is one thing you can do. If the opposing party has a strong position, then it is important to move quickly. At the extreme, you may be able to accept a request or claim without negotiation if it is impossible to challenge the other party. Managers resist any claim from a trade Union as a matter if reactive routine. Managers will be treated more favorably if they say Yes to the union's proposal on occasions when it is clearly well-founded.

Locate

There are many options when it comes to where to hold a meeting. If the meeting is between managers or employees, in which office should it be held? Should a negotiating meeting with trade unions take place in the offices of management or somewhere neutral like a hotel conference hall?

Experienced negotiators will not care about the location, but it is important for many people to consider how the negotiating environment influences their confidence, attitudes, and behavior. This does not necessarily mean that home territory is the best choice.

An experienced personnel manager in large companies was known for his persuasiveness in meetings with colleagues. His working methods were explained to a new secretary. He replied, "Whenever possible, I meet with other managers. however junior. I make every effort to get them into their offices. Not mine. It makes them feel that I am not being honest with myself. They showed more interest in them. So I set one up!

If the negotiation involves complex issues, it might be useful to hold them at home so that you have easy access to supporting documents. If such negotiations are being held far from home, careful consideration should be given to who the members of the team are and what files they should be kept.

Set-piece, large-scale pay bargaining is done on neutral ground in order to avoid any inferences of advantage one side has over the other. Even at a lower level, it is a good idea for the union to request that the meeting be held outside the company's premises. This shows an open, balanced approach. It's quite likely that the union will suggest using the company's conference space.

Refreshments & Seating

The layout of a negotiation's seats can greatly influence or reflect participants' attitudes. Discussions between people sitting together at a very large table can become more heated than if they sit next to each others in an informal group.

The "across the-table" format is the standard layout for formal bargaining sessions. Each team will take one side with their leaders sitting opposite each other at the centre of the long sides. Many people find it easy to use, as it emphasizes the distinct identities of each side and each holds its territory. However, it encourages a competitive "us and them" style. This makes it not the best format for negotiations that aim to eliminate unnecessary attitudinal differences between parties.

A round table, or a group of comfortable armchairs, is a better option for informal, collaborative interactions.

Ed, the personal manager mentioned in the above example, also explained his style to his secretary about how he organizes the few meetings held in his office. He replied, "If I am telling someone rather that asking:" He continued, "I remain behind my desk. If I don't have them, I always bring them over the coffee table to place them in my deepest armchair. softest armchair. When you're comfortable and tucked into your chair, enjoying a cup or coffee, it is difficult to be belligerent.

Sometimes, even in formal meetings it is possible to devise a more unconventional seating plan.

Management knew that one union official would be aggressive, but the senior shop supervisor was known to be more conciliatory.

Allow the union team to sit first. Instead of facing the union official in the middle, the management leader chose a seat at the table directly opposite the senior-steward.

The union official was often unable to catch the manager's attention during negotiations. The latter, however, was able easily to bring in the senior steward.

Parties hosting negotiations or leading the organization of them if they take place on neutral territory are expected to arrange for refreshments. Part of the formal negotiation ritual is to provide tea and coffee or beer and sandwiches.

Even when two managers meet informally at the same time, the fact that the 'host' does not offer a cup or something during the afternoon or mid-morning may be taken as a significant sign of unfriendliness.

However, a refreshment break can serve more purposes than simply complying with office protocols. If tempers have risen, a break for a cup can help lower the emotional temperature. It can also provide an opportunity to have a quiet conversation with the leaders of each team or between individual 'fixers'. Deceitfully, if timing is possible, refreshments might arrive at the same time as the leader from the opposing team. Nothing is more deflating that the loud clang of cups when the tea trolley opens. A delay in having refreshments can be a way to encourage rapid progress.

The conflicting details of a negotiation between two companies about a supply deal was becoming a major problem. At 1 pm, no decision had been reached on the preliminary point regarding quantity discounts. The team leader for the purchasing company then stated: "We've put on a buffet lunch at 1.15 in another room, but I believe we should reach a decision regarding discounts before breaking, or else we will lose the threads behind our arguments." This tactic was agreed upon by the company's staff before the meeting began. However, they were relaxed about the delay and started to feel more comfortable. By 2.15 the other firm's team was becoming very restless.

Documentation

If yes, how long should minutes or other records be kept of the meeting?

Whom and in what format? This is a crucial point. It is not unusual for a verbal deal to be reached in a negotiating meeting. However, the settlement can fall apart later if the two parties have a different understanding and/or recollection about what was said and the details.

The extreme of minute-keeping is called the verbatim. Here, all the words spoken in negotiations are either tape-recorded and/or written down by shorthand writers. It is used occasionally in collective bargaining. It appears to have been implemented because neither party wanted to accept the other's summary and because of disagreements about who had said which during very long negotiations. The method was expensive and required voluminous paperwork. It also proved to be costly for some participants, as their informal comments were later printed and distributed widely. One example is a comment made by a top employer at a meeting, which was intended to be humorous. He said that the National Union of Teachers annual conferences reminded him of a chimpanzees' tea party. Teachers made accusations that he thought they were better than monkeys, which led to them accusing each other in formal minutes. This did not help in securing a modest pay offer.

In general, however, it is not a good idea to keep verbatim transcripts. An effective negotiation's outcome is what matters most. This includes the actual agreement, not the argumentative toil that has led to it. Therefore, it is worth keeping a detailed written record of who was present, what each side said, and what was ultimately agreed to. This kind of record doesn't require a formal time taker. This type of record does not require a formal minute taker.

A deeper private record might be useful, which can help to document in complex negotiations the differing views or emphases from members of the opposing side. Also, it may provide a note of points raised in discussion that did not appear in the final agreement. It is important to keep this private record as a background tool and not as a secret weapon.

Managers can use informal, managerial negotiations to document the results. They can do this by taking the initiative during the discussion and writing a memo confirming the outcome: "Just a quick note to confirm that yesterday we agreed to...

These are the key points

* Negotiations are influenced primarily by the style and speed of the negotiating team, the composition of their negotiating teams, and the arrangements for seating and refreshments.

* They are able to work in a team spirit but also have the ability to be confrontational.

* A team of three or five is best, except for informal negotiations.

* It is best to avoid negotiations while emotions are high. Delaying for their own sake can be counterproductive.

* Experienced negotiators tend to feel more confident when they are at home. However, for formal negotiations that involve major decisions, it might be beneficial to have a neutral location.

* Seating arrangements can be used either to reinforce a confrontational mode or a collaborative one.

* Refreshments should not be considered a matter of common courtesy. It can be used to help negotiate.

* An official record, however innocuous, of the outcome of negotiations is recommended to allow for a common understanding of what was reached.

Chapter 15: Negotiation Strategies & Tactics For Business/Boardroom & Beyond

In order to be prepared for the most important events of life, there are some basic negotiation principles. These strategies are a compilation and application of what I learned as a CIA Field Agent and FBI Special Agent.

But the strategies you learn here can be applied to all negations, especially in the professional workplace or business world. It's important that you don't take this stuff too seriously. The one-upmanship style of exchanges can sometimes be seen as more of an entertainment than a serious business matter. You can master it and win if you do it right and in the right spirit.

Logrolling

Logrolling, a practice used in many high-ranking positions such as politics, is something that is routinely done every day. It's the practice or exchanging favors. It's also known as 'quid proquo' and is very common in the context of legislation voting within parliamentary bodies around the world.

During my time in the FBI and CIA I had my fair share. In office politics, it is a form of currency. But in the field, it's a common behavior. However, it can be an extremely powerful strategy in a negotiation if you play your card right. The idea is to make a variety of requests to each side. Some of these are extremely important but many others are less. This will allow you to maneuver and be seen to be making concessions about things that were not so important to you. You should at least be able to match the other person regarding what they are willing to let go. If you're genuine, this will be a great way to establish empathy in the relationship you want to foster.

Moving Personnel

I mentioned a story from 'Confidence. An Ex-SPY's Guide' where I had the opportunity to fill in for some of the guys who were taken away during an interview with a suspect. It was during my early years at the FBI. It was more an interrogation type interaction than negotiation but the principles still apply. It is more of the "good cop/bad cop" scenario you see in movies or on TV.

This theory states that switching the person actually negotiating can allow you to have a slightly different view of the discussion and possibly push things your way. This works well if you have someone you know who can do the same type of questioning as you. First, you can try your approach and if that doesn't work, then you can switch to your partner. If things are getting really difficult, the new negotiator might even consider starting from scratch.

Positive negotiation or interactions are, as I suggested before, built on positive emotional interaction between the individuals involved. This can also be played as a team game. You should have at least one negotiator for these meetings if you have the ability to do so. Your partner might be able to strike a chord with you in the meeting while you can't or vice versa. It's all about experimentation.

Set the Agenda

Just like the offer-biasing principle, setting and controlling the agenda of a negotiation can play a crucial role in how the actual interaction proceeds. This is because you can control the order and outcome of any discussion. You must think carefully about how people will feel at any particular point.

"Negotiation can be a giving and taking process. However, being in control of the entire process is key to your success."

(Celso Cukierkorn)

It is a good idea to include the least important or irrelevant items at the beginning of the discussion. Everyone will be more fresh and better able analyze the topic. These first points of contention will go either your way or not. But if you've planned things properly, it shouldn't matter that much as they are points that are neither here nor elsewhere for you.

The key is not to waste mental energy analyzing them yourself. Let others do that. When the other party is tired and mentally exhausted, your goal will be to save that critical analyzing juice so you can focus on the important points. It is not your intention for them to think clearly. They will likely be more inclined to make concessions because they won't be thinking as clearly.

This applies only if you have full control of the meeting or agenda. You will still need to be cognizant of these factors if you do not. To win the points you need, it is crucial to use your mental energy wisely in long and complicated negotiations. It is possible to create a pre-planned exit strategy if things aren't going as well. You can easily come up with your own.

Buying Time

If none of your strategies are working, you have one option: Intentionally stalling. This is buying time when things aren't going as planned. This can be useful in two ways. It can help you get out a tight spot if it is hard to decide what you should agree to in a negotiation. This can also work well if you know that the other party is limited by a deadline. If they delay the discussion, they could be forced to partially or completely concede important points.

Never be afraid asking to be excused to go to the bathroom so you can regroup and count down the seconds to add pressure to the other party. However, buying time can be much more discreet than leaving the area if needed. This can sometimes anger the opposite side and do more harm than good.

Sometimes, I found myself in situations that made it impossible to leave the table for complex negotiations undercover in CIA. This is because serious crime bosses won't allow it. In these cases, I would simply work on a point that was of little importance to me while mulling over another more important one that would be next. It is important to keep the tension at a reasonable level so that it doesn't become counterproductive.

Like all the other tactics in this book and others it may take years to perfect the strategies. It is a good idea to take a few moments off of your daily life in order to learn how to manage the pressure when it is not.

Inside Man

This tactic is borrowed directly from intelligence playbook. In some situations, it may be possible and even beneficial to ask for the help of an outsider to assist you in your negotiations.

I was the Portuguese station chief during the 2000s. I was in Rio de Janeiro and Sao Paulo for many years working on intelligence regarding drug cartels originating from the Amazon. Although there are subtle differences with the Brazilian dialect and the native Portuguese dialect, I found them similar enough to be able handle the Lisbon job.

About one year into my time in the field, I was given the task of bringing an end to an organization that stole millions of Euros from the local exchange. They used a sophisticated algorithm to arbitrage over 50 points per day across a variety stocks and indices. The speed of their quotes was faster than the general market. While it was only a handful, very intelligent men were behind the system. However, international markets were aware of their activities.

This is a gray zone that many US quantitative and higher frequency traders exploit. But, back then, this kind of trading was still very young and considered illegal by Europeans. It also had an adverse effect on the stock price of smaller US companies and Asian commodities companies, in which we held a large stake.

It was difficult for local law enforcement to pinpoint exactly where the group's machines were located or gather sufficient evidence to pursue them. It took me several long months to discover the solution. However, once I realised that these guys needed a particular type of fiber optical cable to enable their super-high speed computers and data streams to function properly, I was able to identify how to get there. I effectively put a halt on any local dealers that supply this cable within the area and made sure to train another operative, which we will call Jake, who was also in my team at the moment to act as a free-lance hardware supplier for the type of organization.

Although initially they were cautious about my guy, they eventually closed down their operation for a few weeks to prevent detection. But greed and impatience quickly overtook them. They decided to ask Jake for his help, but the drop off points weren't always located where their trading stations were. It took him 3 months to convince them.

He also threatened to end his supply of the cable if they didn't. The game of blackmail does not end there. He eventually reached an agreement and installed the cable on their computers near the exchange. They were unaware that Jake was actually downloading all trading data from one of their main sites. These guys were shut down immediately, it was obvious.

But I am not suggesting that you must go to great lengths in order to penetrate an organization with which you are trying to negotiate. However, it does illustrate my point. It is possible to make friends with someone in another department and get information about their bosses before you sit down for an important interview. Also, be mindful of any colleague who seems very willing and eager to help you at the time of a crucial negotiation.

Sequential Conversion

This strategy is somewhat similar in nature to the one described above regarding enlisting other people's help. But it's done in a slightly new way. When you need to win the trust of a group of people, it is better to do so one by one. If you are able to do this with success, it will be more difficult to use but will result in more positive outcomes.

The idea is to be able to easily and reasonably convert one person into your way of thinking. You can use any of the empathy-inducing tactics described in this guide or other books. Once you have done this, you can work your way up the list of opposition negotiators and bring them all on board. When you do everything correctly, each of the people that you positively convert will help you in your efforts for the next. This will create an aggregation effect which exponentially increases the effectiveness of your efforts. You are creating a group of people.

As part of a team you can negotiate with your organization. Once you identify the person who would most support your interests, go after them intelligently until you bring everyone on board. Make sure you do your homework to match the personalities of your team with those of the opposition.

Tactical Leaking

Information is definitely the most important commodity in negotiations. There is a fine distinction between spying, and legitimate information collection. This was clearly an occupational hazard. But there is another strategy to gather intel that can be applied to the buildup to a crucial negotiation. It is known as tactical leak.

However, the information "leaked" does not have to be misleading. It may be something accurate, but information you would rather the other side concentrate on without distracting them away from something more crucial. This strategy works best when the leaks are not intended and unknow to the people or organizations that made them. This will make the other party feel confident and secure, as they now have full access to the intel.

This is something that intelligence agencies and government do all the time. It has gotten to the point that there are entire departments at Langley and field stations dedicated to deciphering whether the intel was genuinely leaked, or intentionally placed in their hands by someone who wants it.

Leakage of information can be a smart and effective strategy, provided it is used carefully. Your counterparty believing they have an advantage over you in a negotiation is one of the best things. However, if they get it wrongly they could be severely handicapped. This is because they will likely be more focused on what they have received than on potential critical issues they can better prepare for.

It's important to make this information public as discretely possible. Sometimes, it is best to have a conversation overheard, or to confess to someone in the corridor. Documents left out of place. You might be surprised at the things you may have in your possession, which could make it easier for the other side to get the information they need.

Record

This strategy can be used in conjunction with the tactical leaking methods I have already described. Both are designed to release information to the opposite side that would normally be hidden. They are both performed prior to the key negotiation session as a sort of preparation play. This tactic is often used by governments and political negotiators in situations where an impasse is reached and some degree of "back channeling" is necessary to help move the matter along.

There are subtle differences. The best way to tell someone what you want is to ask them if you are able "off the records" or "speak with confidentiality". This will allow you to share the information directly, but not in a formal manner. You won't tell them anything that you don't wish to be mentioned during your main negotiation session. It is impossible to know whether it will remain private.

However, it can be a very effective way to increase empathy between the parties. If done correctly, it's a gesture of trust that can be reciprocated.

People will often use the "off the records" tactic as well to get information for their own purposes. It's an exchange of information and feelings. You can say "Look Stephen, this would obviously remain confidential but is he actually contemplating accepting it or is he just stalling?". Again, this is a feeling out process. Even though you are engaged in an empathic interchange of trust, the information they might be giving to you could still be what you want to hear. You should pay attention to their vocal tone and visual cues to understand if they are lying. This will be discussed in more detail in "Body Language. An ex-SPY's guide". You will need to trust your instincts. Once you feel comfortable with this method, continue practicing it with the others until you get a better understanding.

This chapter can be read in under one day. However, it's worth going back to each principle or tactic to learn them individually. Once you have mastered the principles and tactics, you will be able to practice implementing them. These are complicated techniques that can only be learned with practice.

Once you have mastered some of the strategies, you will be able to stack them until you start acting like a top-ranking negotiation strategist when you need to make business deals and negotiate boardroom meetings. Keep in mind that it's a game and not something to be taken too seriously.

Chapter 16: Open Negotiations

"Let us never fear to negotiate." John F. Kennedy

Congratulations! You did a great job during the interview process. They are extremely excited to have your on their team. It is common for people to relax at this point, but this is when they need to focus on their game and strike. Tens to thousands of dollars can be resolved in one phone call or meeting. You should get as much as you can. The opening offer is so vital that it deserves its own breakdown.

Before we begin this stage of negotiations, let me remind you of two key facts. First, it's fair and reasonable to negotiate your wages. Second, negotiation is expected. These two points may not be obvious but many people aren't willing to negotiate, as we discussed at the beginning. You should be comfortable asking for more. There is nothing wrong with asking. Many companies have a bumper negotiation room where people can ask for more. Don't let the bumper room pass you by. It doesn't matter if you can't make more money. Although it might be the highest-paid, you should not accept it without at minimum trying to get more.

While job offers come in many forms, they are all basically treated the same. It will be at the end, by email, over the phone, or in person. These situations are similar but we will show you how to handle them all. Do not accept the first offer.

We will begin with the most popular way to receive your offer. It is possible that they allowed you to accept the phone call. If they didn't, it will go to voicemail. Wait until you are in a better spot to call back. Do not negotiate while you are waiting at the grocery or at your kid's soccer games. However, you will want to call back as soon a possible. I recommend that you have your resume along with your salary research notes. You can always refer to these documents quickly when you aren't at home. These information can be found in any folders and binders that you bring to interview. You never know when it might come in handy.

It does not matter whether you answer the phone or call back, but it is important to be friendly in your opening. It is okay to apologize if they missed your call. Talk to the person you are speaking to about past relationships and try to maintain a friendly conversation. You will hear them say that they loved having you and would like to have you join the team. At this point, they should inform you about the salary. If they do not, thank them and then ask for the exact amount. You can simply say the following.

"That is so great! What is the average salary for this position?

There's no need to brag about it, this phone call is all business! It is possible that they may not be completely honest and ask how much money you are interested in getting paid. This is more annoying than anything. But we have already discussed this and we will reuse the technic. Ask them for the typical salary range for the job, or to determine the fair compensation. You should not give out your first number. They can reply in any number of ways, including giving you your number, giving you a wide range or even double-down. As they have no other options, we will continue to use the high number as a response. To make sure you are covered, you will be able to say your salary and three weeks of paid vacation. It is possible for you to give an answer but it cannot be rejected so make sure that you include as much as possible. Once they have received your answer, they will either counter or give you a written offer. After you have covered this issue via email and at interview's end, we will talk about what to do next.

Sometimes an email may be enough to offer you a job. It would contain the same words as over the telephone, thanking for you coming in and asking you to join the team. It is unlikely that someone will email you asking for the number. It is harder to negotiate by email. If they ask for your number, use the same handle that we used above to try and get it from them. You can also offer to give them call to discuss. Your email must be professionally written. You should spell check your email and ensure the formatting is consistent. If you don't have the time, get someone else to go over it. You might be overwhelmed by your nerves. The same greeting should be used as the opening message for their email. If they reply with "Hi Jessica", then you should reply with "Hi Billy". You should not rush to respond. This email is not a telephone call. Make sure you take your time, and write a great response. If they do give the number, after some back & forth, you will have your opening deal or you gave it.

Finally, we have the facetoface offer. This is often the most complex, but it includes all the necessary parts for a phone or email opening. This can occur at the end of an interview. This is a good sign about how your interview went. This is more common in small corporations, which have a smaller number of decision makers. They will need to go through the process again with a larger corporation before making an offer. An exception to this rule is when you visit for a followup interview, particularly if it's your third or forth interview. These might be for final approval interviews and a final filter in order to verify that you are not a liability. You might be offered an offer if they have already made it clear to you. This is a sign of their genuine interest in you, which can be financially advantageous for them. They have already invested a lot and see you as an employee of the company.

Other possibilities include being called back in to accept the position in-person. This is more common for higher-paying positions that are also higher up in the company. They desire to have personal contact with their manager for this critical position. It may feel more difficult to accept the situation in this case, but don't let this get to you. They invited and expected you to accept the position. There is no reason to feel weak about salary negotiation. Don't allow them to psyche yourself out. You will always be treated the same face-to face, no matter how you got there.

The main difference between face to face offers and previous examples is that there is a higher likelihood of you accepting it. Emotions may be strained from an interview or you might feel uncomfortable asking for more money. This is the time to focus on the details and get the money you want. Maintain the mindset that negotiation is acceptable and is to be expected.

Don't make the first deal. We have discussed several ways that you can get it back to them so they can provide the number. This is how you made it. Now, make sure to get your money back. It doesn't matter how much you are dealt, you must remain calm. Maintaining a friendly and light-hearted relationship with your partner is key to maintaining a great rapport. Don't be afraid to ask for help.

This is where your body language can be crucial. Don't slouch and drop your shoulders.

Believe in yourself, and let your potential shine through. They are beautiful, so look in their eyes. I don't want you to be too creepy. Either you have to accept the first offer, and the negotiations will end, or they will counter and make their offer.

No matter how we got here, we have our first offer form the possible employer. Now you can prepare for your response and close of negotiations. Let's make sure you maximize your offer.

Chapter 17: #1 Transformation Strategy

Strategy 1 - Developing self-confidence and positive thoughts

Self-confidence can be defined as a mental state that is related to how you view yourself. When you are confident you feel happy and positive about yourself.

These people, who are confident and positive in life, tend to have a greater appreciation for others and respect themselves. They are willing and able to face any challenges that life throws at them, as well as overcome failures.

They don't mind overcoming obstacles and enjoy the challenge of pursuing their goals. They treat success with dignity and have fun celebrating it.

These people are not filled with negative emotions but instead use their energy to be positive.

It is possible to build self-confidence. You must learn how to attain Self-Confidence.

When a person is treated badly or has had their self-esteem and confidence shaken, or they see failures in important areas of life, they can become very demoralized. At any stage of life, self-esteem or self confidence can be earned.

Self-confidence can have many benefits. You will see the positive in everyone around you.

Self-Esteem has many benefits. They include positive self-esteem, being open to taking risks, feeling confident, and being able achieve your goals quickly.

A person who has self-confidence can be positive and not allow negative thoughts to lower his Self-Esteem. These people are able to achieve new heights and don't get discouraged when they fail.

In fact, his positive outlook helps him transform negative behavior into something positive and makes it easy for him to feel comfortable and confident.

You can consult your counselor if depression or feeling low.

Self-Esteem can be measured by how confident you are in your work or act.

There are many factors that affect the level of Self-Esteem. It is dependent on your life experiences and upbringing.

Most people in society don't want to be assigned a job by someone nervous, slow, or fumbling.

On the other side, you might accept any proposal from someone who clearly explains his work, or answers all questions in public and is able to answer them quickly, and most importantly, who freely admits when they don't know something.

Self-confident people increase confidence in all people. It also inspires confidence and trust in others.

A confident person can easily overcome the negative thoughts, and achieve success. Self-confidence is something that every person should possess in their life. It keeps people happy and gives you the feeling of greatness within yourself.

Your behavior, body language and the way you speak can all influence your Self-Confidence. Your belief in what you do will make you the most popular person.

Strategy 2 - Mind Control

Mind control has been a mystery to many for years. Mind control power is usually displayed through entertainment and magic, with some even claiming that they have been tricked by people controlling their minds.

Mind control may be described as the ability to place another person under your control. You may be able to learn the technique on your own, but the power of your subconscious mind is far greater than your conscious mind.

You may be one of those people who are impressed by magicians that claim to control the mind, or you just want to know more about it. Here are some methods you might find useful.

Mind control can be achieved through imagination, visualization, or keen observation. The subconscious mind is the best tool for controlling your mind. However, it can also be used to control your thoughts. These simple techniques will help you increase your power over your subconscious mind.

Learn hypnosis. Hypnosis can be used for overcoming fear and phobias. The ability to hypnotize others is a great way to learn mind control skills. You must learn the correct way to do hypnosis in order to be able apply it.

Building trust and a sense of confidence is another method that will help you reach your goals. It is possible to influence others by gaining their trust and confidence. Being able to control others is no easy task. It is possible to persuade, influence and convince others by building trust. This will help you begin your mind control techniques.

Brainwave technologies are another way to help you control the mind of others. However, experts and professionals can also help you to master these techniques. Your subconscious is an integral part of your ability to use your mind. However, you must also be responsible enough to not misuse this ability.

Donald Trump targeted his audience when he ran for office and played to them during campaigns. He didn't care who liked, supported, or favored him. Trump was aware that he was not participating in a popularity contest and was only catering for a few voters who believed in his ideology. He was not dismissive of popularity polls or expert opinions. It was his belief that your brand should not appeal to everyone. Instead, your brand should address the concerns and needs of your audience in a relevant and impactful way. He became the voice of disillusioned

Republicans that were hopeful about the White House's return. Trump unafraidly and candidly shares the feelings of his audience. Identify your target market, discuss their concerns, then present solutions. Isn't that the essence of savvy marketing?

Strategy 3 - Polishing your Communication and Persuasion Skills

Persuasion can be a powerful influence weapon. It's the art of persuading others to follow your path and get what you want. No matter whether you are motivating people for sales or delivering an address, your ability communicate effectively with others will affect your ability to persuade them.

To ignite your passion for persuasion and ignite your passion, you need to sharpen your communication abilities. It is important to remember that communication and being able to present oneself are two of the most essential skills in business today.

Here are some tips to improve your communication skills and persuasive abilities.

If you communicate and persuade effectively, you will always see the results.

Your ability to communicate effectively with others is essential in business. Communicating effectively is the main skill you must develop. It is vital that you communicate effectively in order to ensure your company and sales success. There are many persuasive methods to communicate well, one of which is to paint word images.

What do you think are painting words pictures?

You can touch your prospects to see his thoughts and feel their emotions. To get to grips with his mind, you need to stimulate the imagination. Because our brains think more in pictures and less words,

It's just like reading a lengthy story. Most people stop reading after five to 10 pages, as they are unable to see anything but words.

Compare these books with more photos that are more likely to motivate readers.

To persuade people, have them read your book with additional pictures. This will keep their attention on what you are saying and help them feel emotionally connected.

Strategy 4 - Think Creatively

Being creative is a way to improve persuasion skills. Although it's not the book, but the principle that can help you persuade better, these principles should not be ignored as they are the foundation for your persuasion skill.

Here are some ways you can increase your persuasion abilities using creativity.

Credibility can help build trust and confidence. It will also help to increase your charisma, physical attractiveness, and overall credibility. This can attract your customers or clients to listen to what you have to say.

The second is to use positive, tactful tone throughout your persuasion.

This can make it easier to negotiate with mature clients and customers who are intelligent, smart, and mature. You should show respect and sincerity to them. When you start talking to them, be direct and polite. It also includes presenting ideas to them. Present one idea at a given time, to be clear.

In addition to presenting your idea clearly, you must also present strong evidence supporting your argument. Think of creative ways to get more information. This will help you persuade customers and clients. This means that your arguments will be tailored to them. Ask your question as if they have preconceived opinions about what you're selling.

Perhaps it is not enough to simply state your feelings clearly. You must go deeper to touch the most vulnerable part in a person. You can use your emotional appeal to help you get to know your customers or clients better. Once you have this insight, you can then mold everything.

Persuasion requires a lot of work. Before you can apply the skills in your business or sales, it will take a lot time.

Don't assume your prospects will need you

Do you remember ever trying to persuade someone and having a hard time because he didn't know what he wanted. This is most often the problem with all persuaders since their prospects may not know what they want.

Perhaps you already know how to get your prospects to agree to your sales. How to grab their attention. If you are faced with a prospect that doesn't know what you want, here is some advice.

It is best to assume your prospects don't know much about the products you are trying to sell. You can ask them a lot after you have won their trust. It is important that your questions relate to the product or product similar to yours. When you ask them more questions, it is important to keep your eyes on the prospect and listen carefully to what they have to say. This allows you to gather information from your prospects that will help you determine what they need.

There are many ways to understand your customers and clients better. To be able understand their exact needs, there are many more things you should learn.

It is possible to make more sales by improving your ability to establish a rapport with your customers and clients. Rapport refers to being able and willing to work with others. The best way to be in sync is to mimic your prospects' body language or gestures, and keep eye contact.

By building a rapport with your clients, you can modify your language to make them feel valued. You'll also be able sell less to help them buy more.

It is important to remember that if your prospect needs are not being met, you will waste your time and possibly lose your sales.

Following the advice I gave you above can help reduce your sales cycles.

Strategy 5 - Use Power and Influence in a responsible manner

The most important skill you have in your life is the ability to persuade others and influence them so that they can help you achieve your goals.

You can influence people to make your life easier. Because you have people around you who are always ready to help you and support, this will help you get more done in life.

If you can influence another person, you're not only a leader but also someone who inspires confidence and supports others.

It is impossible to fail with the support and guidance of people around you.

Your ability to influence people and to use your power can help you achieve high goals.

This will also make it possible for others to support you in every aspect of your life.

This can help you be a leader in the community or a boss at work.

There are those who don't have the persuasive power to influence others and at all times of their lives.

They are anxious people and cannot express themselves with poise. It is difficult for them in their lives to succeed.

They're not sure what they're doing, and that leads to failure. They should be taught how influence works so they can achieve success.

Knowing the difference between helping others and taking advantage of others is essential to your ability to do your job well. This ability can be measured by the person's ability or inability to influence others.

Being unable to convince people is a sign that you don't work for people.

Motivation is key to persuasion. It is essential to be able and able to persuade others with your influence and quality.

Studying people around you is essential to be able understand their motivations and then trying to inspire them.

Confident people are easy to convince. Motivation comes in many forms. Satisfaction does not come easily.

It is human nature for us to seek more. If we can satisfy our other half by letting them know how we achieved higher success, then they can be stimulated to do the same.

Influence can also be used to your advantage. This means you can show your personality and work in their style. This would mean that they would work for your cause and will be doing what you want. Also, they have been affected by you power and have been persuaded to work for what you want.

This is called leverage, as you're only directing work style and managing work while others do the rest.

Management is when you get the work done by others. It is easy to reach the position of manager. However, in order to inspire people to follow your lead and work for you, it is necessary to be able to convince them.

Once you have this ability, you will be an expert manager. Assigning duties is enough. They will accept responsibility because they feel impressed.